THE

GALAPAGOS

ISLANDS

THE

GALAPAGOS

ISLANDS

*The Essential Handbook for
Exploring, Enjoying & Understanding
Darwin's Enchanted Islands*

Marylee Stephenson

The Mountaineers/Seattle

The Mountaineers: Organized 1906 "... to explore, study, preserve, and enjoy the natural beauty of the Northwest."

3 2 1 0 9
5 4 3 2 1

Published by The Mountaineers
306 Second Avenue West, Seattle, Washington 98119
Published simultaneously in Canada by Douglas & McIntyre, Ltd.,
1615 Venables Street, Vancouver, B.C. V5L 2H1

Manufactured in the United States of America
Edited by Richard C. May
Cover design by Betty Watson
Layout by Amy Hines
Cover photographs: Top: Waved albatross. Inset: Male frigate bird with fully inflated gullar pouch. Center: Tortoise in the Tortoise Reserve. Bottom: Blue-footed boobies
Frontispiece: Blue-footed booby and downy chick

Library of Congress Cataloging in Publication Data

Stephenson, Marylee.
    The Galapagos Islands: the essential handbook for exploring, enjoying &
understanding Darwin's enchanted islands/by Marylee Stephenson.
        p.   cm.
    ISBN 0-89886-225-6
    1. Natural history — Galapagos Islands — Guide-books.   2. Galapagos
Islands — Description and travel — Guide-books.   I. Title.
QH198.G3S73   1989   89-38934
508.866′5 — dc20   CIP

Contents

Appendices   149

Regarding Island Names

Virtually all of the Galapagos Islands have been known by more than one name. This book follows current Ecuadorian usage, with a couple of common exceptions. Alternate names of major islands are shown in parentheses in the Table of Contents and respective chapter headings.

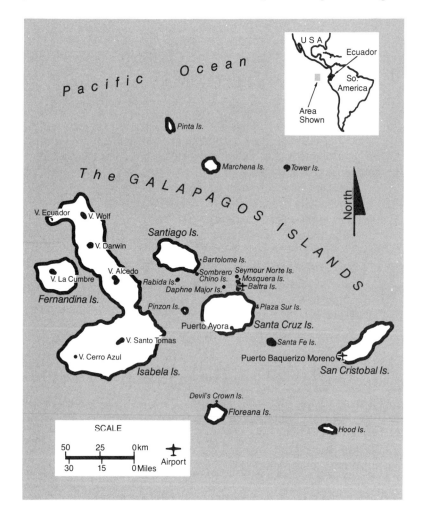

Acknowledgments

The Galapagos are a very important place for me, and there have been a number of people who have contributed to my enjoyment of these Islands. They and others also played an instrumental role in my being able to complete this book.

In recording my debt, I would like to start with those who assisted in my visits there. First, there are Isabel Chaput of Club Aventure in Montreal, and my traveling companion, Pamela Sachs. Then there are Fiddi Angermeyer and Judy Carvalhal, of the yachts *Cachalote* and *Andando*. Ingrid Versteeg of Galapagos Holidays, Toronto, made my latest trip possible, when all other arrangements were falling apart. The guides of each of the trips were very important to increasing my appreciation of the Islands. On my first trip, Diego Andrade provided a superb example of the skills of the auxiliary guide. Jose (Pepe) Salcedo, then a naturalist-guide and now captain of the motor/sailor *Sulidae*, brought voluminous knowledge and a most gracious and accommodating manner to my second voyage. The auxiliary guide Bolivar assisted on my latest trip, soldiering on, sometimes in difficult circumstances.

In my preparation for an article on the Islands, I was able to interview a number of scientists at the Charles Darwin Research Station. Those interviews certainly fed into the contents of this book, in terms of both general background and specific facts. I would like to thank Dr. Friedeman Koster, then Director of the Station, Sylvia Harcourt. Bob Reynolds, Gary Robinson, and Bruce Barnett. Also, I would like to thank Fausto Cepeda, then Superintendent of the Galapagos National Park, for discussing the operations of the Park with me.

Finally, in my direct work on the book, I am indebted to G.T. Corley Smith, past Secretary General of the Charles Darwin Foundation for his comments on the above-mentioned article and for providing me with a virtually complete collection of the Research Station's journal, *Noticias de Galapagos*, from which he has just recently retired as editor.

Ingrid Versteeg reviewed the travel parts of the manuscript and made many helpful comments, based on her years of work in bringing the Galapagos to the visitor, and vice versa. To me, she represents the finest in enlightened approaches to tourism to the Islands.

Michael Jackson, author of the excellent *Galapagos, a Natural History Guide* (University of Calgary Press, 1985), reviewed the entire manuscript for me, and was extremely helpful and generous with his comments. The maps were prepared by Monica Jackson, and I thank her for her goodwill under tight deadlines.

As the reader will see in Part II, I have quoted often from journals of other visitors to the Islands. Aside from Darwin himself, these people are all friends of mine and I would like to thank them here. They are Graeme Gibson, and Elizabeth Greene and my intrepid traveling companions and nephews, Skeeter and Cricket Griesman.

The family of Nicole Proulx and Andre Burelle made it possible for me to write the second part of the book by giving me an excellent workspace and the use of their computer.

Naturally, though I received so much help from all these people, any errors in the book are exclusively attributable to me. 🌸

SAFETY CONSIDERATIONS

The fact that a trip or area is described in this book is not a representation that it is a safe one for you or your group. This book does not list every hazard that may confront you — and can't, due to changing terrain and weather, and the varying capabilities of different travelers. You must assume responsibility for your own safety when you travel, and must exercise your own independent judgment.

Passion flower ▶

PART I. *Overview*

The Living Laboratory

1

> *What havoc the introduction of any new beast of prey must cause in a country, before the instincts of the indigenous inhabitants have become adapted to the stranger's craft or power.*
>
> Darwin, *Voyage of the Beagle*

For nearly a century and a half, since Darwin's visit in 1835, the Galapagos Islands have been recognized as a living laboratory for the study of biological evolution. Much more recently, it has become clear that these exotic islands provide two more lessons about life: how easily it can be destroyed, and how difficult it is to reverse or even slow that destruction.

The Galapagos are an archipelago, volcanic in origin, located about 1000 kilometers (621 miles) directly west from Ecuador. They straddle the Equator, extending 220 kilometers (137 miles) in a north–south direction. There are five islands of over 500 square kilometers (193 square miles) in area, two islands between 100 and 200 square kilometers (38 and 76 square miles) and about 15 smaller ones, most of which may be visited. There are also dozens of tiny islets that are part of the whole collection that is the archipelago. The smallest island that people visit is Plaza Sur, only .13 square kilometers (.05 square mile).

The Islands are a National Park of Ecuador. Over 85 percent of the land mass and all of the waters are preserved and protected as a National Park. There are several settlements in the archipelago, the largest being Puerto Ayora on Santa Cruz, and Puerto Baquerizo Moreno on San Cristobal. The total population is about 6000. The total number of visitors to the Islands in 1987 (the latest figures) was about 25,000. More than one-third of these were Ecuadoreans.

Today's visitor is very much a part of Galapagos history, for tourism is both one of the greatest threats to, and best hope for, the preservation of the quality of life of the Islands. To understand that statement more fully, and to fit visitors right into their own "ecological niche" in this marvelous environment, it's necessary first to look briefly at the natural and human history of the Galapagos.

Far-flung islands are particularly appropriate places to study specific biological processes because their flora and fauna are less diverse than those of the older and larger continental land masses. Islands of fairly

◀ **Tree cactus forest on lowland trail of Santa Fe Island**

Female vermilion flycatcher

recent volcanic origin, like the Galapagos (considered to be "only" 3 million years old), have had less time for soil to develop. If the lack of time is accompanied by extremely high or very low rainfall in the area, or by extremes of temperature (as would be the case near either pole), then soil development is further retarded. Poor soil means less plant development, and hence fewer life forms that can be supported on the land.

Just as the problems of, and opportunities for, survival on far-off islands are distinctive, or even unique, so may be the life forms that evolve in such isolation. Species that are found only in a specific locale, such as the Galapagos, are said to be *endemic*. The Galapagos are famous for their endemic species. These products of the evolutionary process are a constant source of fascination for the visitor, whether tourist or scientist.

The fact that islands are, by definition, a distance from a mainland mass means that there are obstacles to the transport of animal or plant life to the island's shores. Some islands, such as the Galapagos, are far from a continental land mass. The life forms found on such islands are ones that can withstand the long period of exposure to sun, wind and salt water that the accidental journey entails. Life forms that make a landfall, particularly early in an island's history, may find poor or no soil, little or no fresh water, and few other plants or animals to provide sustenance. They may find no others of their own species, which would prevent reproduction (unless fertilization had already taken place). Plants that rely on cross-fertilization for their reproduction face the same problem.

Such obstacles to transportation, sustenance and reproduction can result in a "skewing" of the types and relative proportions of different life forms found on islands. On the Galapagos, for instance, the largest endemic plants are tree-sized composites—relatives of the sunflower. We are used to seeing sunflowers, daisies and their relatives nodding in the breeze in open fields, supported by stems of a few centimeters in diameter and having a height of half a meter at most, except for the cultivated varieties that can be two meters in height. But in the Galapagos the Scalesia "trees" have woody and pithy stems that allow them to achieve considerable height, though they are not true trees, with real bark and tree-type circulatory systems. The Scalesia trees were able to land in the Galapagos because the seeds of the composite family are airborne, and can be blown for great distances. These trees can achieve great size because, until recently, they were the most successful competitor for the soil that exists on the moist upper slopes of the larger of the Galapagos Islands — they could reach their full potential, as it were.

In the animal world of the Galapagos, the predominant forms are reptiles. Reptiles can endure long periods without food or fresh water, and could be transported easily from the South American mainland on the rafts of soil and vegetation that are carried by river and ocean currents out to

Lava lizard on volcanic rock

sea. The giant tortoise and the land and marine iguanas have come to characterize these Islands, both in terms of biological distinctiveness and of capturing the public imagination.

Amphibians and mammals cannot withstand weeks of baking sun and little or no food. So endemic land mammals are few, and native amphibians are non-existent on the Islands.

There are only two types of terrestrial mammals—two species of bat and two species of rat. There were seven species of rat, but the other five became extinct because of the overwhelming competition for food and space that came from introduced black rats (*Rattus rattus*).

Of the Galapagos mammals, the visitor will be most aware of the marine species—the fur seals, sea lions and several species of whales and porpoises that occur in these waters.

Birdlife is abundant in the Galapagos. Here again, as with the plant and other animal life, the "island effect" can be seen. Since birds can fly great distances, many of the sea-going ("pelagic") species are very evident, but few are found *only* in the Galapagos. Boobies, frigate birds, tropic birds, pelicans, shearwaters, petrels and noddies are frequently encountered. They are generally the same species found hundreds or even thousands of miles away on other land masses. The waved albatross, though it patrols thousands of square kilometers of ocean for food, is interesting in terms of endemicism. It easily travels great distances, yet almost all of the breeding pairs in the world breed on one tiny Galapagos island, Hood. So the waved albatross, like most of the other pelagic species, is what is known as an *indigenous* species. But they are not an endemic species, found exclusively there.

The endemic ocean-going bird species are much more limited in range. There are a few thousand penguins unique to the Islands, as well as two species of gull, and the flightless cormorant. The penguins, gulls and cormorants do not stray far from their Island home. Thus, however each of these species may have arrived there, they have been confined to the area ever since and have evolved into distinct species over great lengths of time.

Proportionately more species of land-based birds are endemic to the Islands. Reasons for this are complex; but they, too, are linked to the great distances between the island and the mainland.

However, despite the difficulties of transportation to the island and the problems of reproduction, there is a potential advantage: those who do survive may find little competition from other organisms. A plant that had to struggle for enough nutrients, light and space may find a surfeit of each on a distant island little colonized by other plants, or at least by plants with very similar requirements for survival.

A bird that formerly had to fly long distances over water, and then dive ceaselessly just to get enough food, may find rich pickings right next to the shore. A finch-like bird that fed on a very few kinds of seeds may learn how

Tree ferns and Galapagos visitor ▶

Darwin's finch

to feed on insects, though in its place of origin that food was taken by woodpeckers. An animal that was preyed upon by carnivores may find itself in a location where these predators do not exist. And over hundreds of thousands of years, the newcomer may lose its genetically based wariness of the unfamiliar.

The processes of evolution, of the mechanisms of natural selection, are too complex to elaborate upon here. But results that are typical of evolutionary processes can be very evident in distant islands like the Galapagos.

Gigantism is common in these circumstances, and the Islands do support huge land tortoises, and giant Scalesia and ferns the size of trees. Flightlessness is common; the Galapagos Islands have the flightless cormorant. Also common is a proliferation of closely related species, filling distinct ecological niches only a few meters in altitude or a valley or mountaintop away. The well-known 13 species of "Darwin's finches," believed to have come from a common finch-like ancestor and now each distinct in its habits and appearance, are examples of this process. Some species are found in only a few places, others in many ; some overlap in their range. The four species of mockingbird endemic to the archipelago tell a similar story. And the fearlessness of the animals in the Galapagos in the face of introduced threats, like humans, is evidently also characteristic of animal life on distant islands.

This formation of new and different species of plant or animal life is called *adaptive radiation*. The new species adapt to fill newly available niches, or adapt in order to fill previously available niches in a new way.

Visitors to the Islands will see examples of this process at every turn. The guides are well-trained to point out the distinct characteristics of the plants and animals and to identify those that are endemic or indigenous. Introduced species, plant and animal, will be very evident; so too will be their generally negative impact.

The behavioral distinctiveness will also be very clear; the calm acceptance of human visitors by the animal life is a major factor in making a trip to the Galapagos a truly impressive and moving experience.

But these same qualities of far-flung islands can be the source of their extreme vulnerability. Shallow soil can be swept away in moments during torrential rain if the trees that anchored it have been razed for grazing domestic animals. A narrow footpath up a cinder slope quickly widens into a huge trough under the impact of thousands of feet every month. Fearless animals can be killed by the outstretched hand. Predatory animals that have suddenly been introduced to the island can devour eggs laid in sand or in burrows. There is not enough time for a species to evolve new solutions to this new threat.

Today's visitor has come just in time to the Galapagos—in time to see the effects of human interference on biological processes, and just how quickly life can be destroyed. 🐛

Human History

2

Written record of the human history of the Galapagos begins with records of one Fray Tomas de Berlanga, who in 1535 was Bishop of Panama and the highest representative of the Catholic church in the Spanish territories of the Americas. Fray Tomas was sent on a trouble-shooting mission to Peru, under orders from the Holy Roman Emperor, Charles V. Tomas' ship, becalmed off the west coast of South America, drifted to what we now know as the Galapagos. Fray Tomas sent men ashore on several islands to look for desperately needed water. His description of what was seen and done has a familiar ring:

> ... *they found nothing but seals, and turtles, and such big tortoises that each could carry a man on top of itself and many iguanas that are like serpents* ...

> [*on another island*]... *the same conditions prevailed as on the first; many seals, turtles, iguanas, tortoises, many birds like those of Spain, but so silly that they do not know how to flee, and many were caught in the hand. (Hickman, p. 19)*

Much of the human history that followed is similar. People landed to search for water and rarely found it. They saw a place that was quite bizarre and inhospitable. They noticed the fearlessness of the animals and took full advantage of it, for "sport" and for food, which meant mostly tortoise meat.

It was the Spanish for tortoise, "galapagos," that eventually stuck as the name for the Islands. It replaced the earlier "Encantadas," Spanish for "enchanted" or "bewitched." (This name apparently arose out of the baffling and treacherous currents around the Islands, or the peculiar light conditions that made them appear and disappear from a distance, in a mirage-like fashion.)

Early explorers were followed by (or overlapped with) buccaneers. South America and its wealth—real and imagined—were hotly contested by the French, Spanish and English. Naturally, the waters around it were the scene of many struggles for power and booty. The Galapagos provided a hideout for buccaneers, offering them sporadic water supplies and regular supplies of meat. This use of the Islands by pirates continued through much of the 18th century.

◀ Close-up of thorny rosettes on tree cactus

Shell of Pacific marine turtle on egg-laying beach

The 19th century saw the Islands exposed to what was probably the largest and most destructive wave of human visitation—the whalers. The buccaneers certainly slaughtered animal life, and they introduced rats, cats and other highly destructive animals, which went about their own terrible depredations. But for sheer numbers, no other groups were as large as the aggregate numbers of whaling ships and their crews. In one estimate, based upon whaling ship records, there were at least 700 whaling ships plying the Pacific between 1811 and 1844. Any one ship that came to the Islands would take from 100 to 600 tortoises on board. (Another estimate of the rate of depletion: in one 30-year period, over 200,000 tortoises were taken from the Islands.)

The reason why the tortoises were so sought-after was that they provided fresh meat for the long voyages. Tortoises were stacked in the holds and could live as long as a year without food or water. Considering the atrocious quality of food on most sea voyages of the time, the appeal of fresh meat is obvious.

The numbers of tortoises that originally existed on the Islands must have been phenomenal to have withstood this kind of destruction for at least two centuries. But by 1846 there were no tortoises left on Floreana, and those on Rabida and Santa Fe became extinct around that time as well.

The only thing that saved the few remaining tortoises was that the same rapaciousness shown to them was applied to whales. In the mid-1800s whale stocks became so low that the whaling industry virtually collapsed. The visits by whalers to the Galapagos ended by 1865.

Of course, the activities of explorers, buccaneers and whalers brought with them the maritime arm of authority. Naval ships from various countries occasionally visited the Islands, sometimes by accident, sometimes as part of explorations for mapping or for finding dependable locations for water or food.

It was as a part of the English Admiralty's world-wide mapping efforts that Charles Darwin came to the Galapagos for five weeks in 1835. As the naturalist on the *Beagle*, he visited several of the islands. He recounts in some detail the varied characteristics of the wildlife, including the notable fearlessness. His account of his visit in *The Voyage of the Beagle* is quite readable and highly recommended.

On a visit to the home of the administrator of the Islands, Darwin was told that it was possible to tell which island a tortoise came from by noting the differences in the shape of the tortoise's shell, or carapace. This, plus the unique forms of birdlife, seems to have been seminal in the slow evolution of Darwin's own thoughts on the role of natural selection in evolution.

If you have a chance to read the Galapagos section of Darwin's book, you should bring along photocopies of those pages. You will find it is possible to read Darwin's account and travel along in his footsteps here and there. Your actual paths won't necessarily be the same, but you will be seeing parts of the same islands and many of the same plants and animals as he did.

By the time that Darwin arrived on the Islands there had already been some human settlement there. It was of a distinctly depressing sort, however. In 1833, an attempt was made to colonize the Islands with reprieved mutineers from the Ecuadorean army. (As their choice was to serve as colonists or be executed, the level of enthusiasm for the whole project can well be imagined.) Shortly thereafter, another penal colony was established on Floreana. The cruelty of the overseers of the colony became notorious over the nearly 100 years that it continued to exist.

The 19th century saw several more attempts to colonize the Islands in order to extract salt or sulfur, or to grow crops such as sugar cane. None succeeded; and when the end came to most, it was a violent one.

Of course, it must be borne in mind that buccaneers, whalers and colonizers didn't just take from the Island—they gave. This was not out of a spirit of charity, of course, but rather the unknowing and uncaring introduction of a wide variety of foreign plant and animal life. Whalers may come and go, but the goats, cats, rats, fire ants, guava plants, avocado, balsa and coffee they brought with them—all gone wild and taking over the space and food sources of endemic species—are still much in evidence today.

Young booby displaying or begging for food

Toward the end of the 1800s scientific interest in the Islands increased and there were periodic expeditions to the archipelago. Their goals may have been benign (though the "collector mentality" cannot always be seen as such), but their impact on the fragile Galapagos ecosystem was not. The scientists collected specimens in large numbers, often with little or no scientific justification, while the locals readily supplied them with food from rapidly dwindling wildlife resources. Destructive consumption of endangered species by scientists continued until the 1930s.

The vivid accounts of some of the scientists who visited the Islands after the turn of this century led some people, particularly in Norway, to believe that the Galapagos could be another Utopia. A few individuals and families tried to make a go of it, though very few succeeded. There are detailed accounts of these attempts and more won't be recounted here (see Suggested Reading).

There are a few European families in the Islands now. A much larger number of Ecuadorean nationals came for the land that was free to whoever was willing to try farming in the difficult environment.

The Islands continued to deteriorate rapidly in the next several decades as a slowly increasing population quite understandably did all it could to shape the natural environment into one suitable for farming, ranching and village living. Trees were cut to clear grazing land. Open areas were burned by accident or for agricultural reasons, then overtaken by plants that had arrived by accident on boats or had been introduced as potential crops and had spread beyond any farmer's fencing.

The new plants often succeeded too well—sometimes the land wasn't even useful for pasture because such dense thickets were formed that no domestic animals could live among them.

Where ground cover was lost, erosion of sloping land was widespread. It doesn't rain often in the Galapagos. But when it does, usually during El Nino events, it rains in torrents that unmercifully erode unprotected soil.

Wildlife was hunted, including tortoises. And of course, the predations of introduced mammals such as cats, dogs, burros, goats and rats continued unabated. 🐢

Saying No to Destruction **3**

hough much of the early scientific work in the Galapagos was of dubious value, at least in terms of its impact on Island wildlife, the activities of scientists did eventually lead to positive change. Progress has been slow, but is very definitely occurring. However, it has been a very close call, and there are long struggles ahead.

Progress began with the 1935 Galapagos Memorial Expedition, which was composed of an international team of scientists visiting the Islands to commemorate the 100th anniversary of Darwin's visit. Their work was instrumental in focusing the attention of the international scientific community on the Galapagos. The Ecuadorean government passed legislation aimed at the protection of Island wildlife. But there were no "teeth" to the legislation, and any further progress toward conservation was completely interrupted by World War II.

The decline of the 1930s, unchecked by legislation that existed but was not enforced, continued and perhaps even increased as the human population slowly expanded and the populations of introduced plants and animals grew exponentially.

But 1959 saw another landmark in the renewal of the Islands: the 100th anniversary of the publication of Darwin's *The Origin of Species*. That year, the combined efforts of Ecuadorean conservationists and international scientific and conservation groups resulted in the establishment of the two basic building blocks of the renewed Galapagos: the Ecuadorean government declared all of the Islands (exclusive of already-settled areas) to be a National Park, protected from all forms of destructive use; and the Charles Darwin Foundation was incorporated. The Foundation was supported by UNESCO and the International Union for the Conservation of Nature (IUCN), among other groups and individuals, in agreement with the Ecuadorean government. The agreement included authorization for the Foundation to continue as an international body until 1989, when it would become officially Ecuadorean. The mandate of the Foundation (and its staff at the Research Station on Santa Cruz) is to carry on scientific research and to advise National Park staff regarding the conservation of the Islands. They are to act "as twin brothers," as one Station Director told me.

It was not until 1964 that the Research Station actually began to operate in the Islands. Three years later, a National Parks Service was set

◀ **Sea lions relaxing in pools on Mosquera Island**

up, under the direct guidance of the Ecuadorean government. The first Park Superintendent started work in 1972 and over the years small numbers of wardens and patrol boats have been added to the Service.

There are many superb examples of the "twin brother" approach to the conservation of the Galapagos. One is that the Research Station brings its expertise in scientific and conservation matters to the courses which all Park Service guides must take before they are licensed to work on boats. The guides bring that knowledge to the tourist, and make sure that animals are not disturbed, flowers not picked, that shoes are carefully cleaned when leaving any site and boarding the boat (so seeds from one island are not introduced to another); in general, that the Islands are treated with enlightened respect.

The guides also play an important role as a frontline defense against any detrimental changes to the Island environment. As a group, the guides have spent much more time in many more places in the Islands than most of the Research Station scientific staff (unless a scientist has grown up in the

Goats along the trail on Santiago Island

Islands, which is not the usual pattern). Guides are out every day in nearly every corner of the archipelago, and they notice sudden changes like fire, volcanic eruptions, or the approach of destructive introduced animals to previously safe areas. They have also found populations of endangered iguanas and tortoises when no one thought there were any left to be found.

This kind of information is instantly fed into the Station and the Park Service so that immediate reactions can be made, like putting out fires or fencing off delicate areas. It also contributes to long-term study of the situation so that proper decisions can be made about the best long-range responses. The Charles Darwin Research Station has been central to the development of programs of predator control, and of captive breeding and return of threatened species.

Control, much less total eradication, of wild dogs, goats, burros, cats and rats is extraordinarily difficult. There are an estimated 200,000 goats on Santiago alone! (It has been possible to eliminate them, however, on a few of the smaller islands.) Rats remain an intractable problem here, as they are world-wide. The battle against dogs, especially as they endanger the flightless cormorants that nest in the northern part of Isabela, is so far making slow progress. Cats and burros still roam freely on the many islands they inhabit.

But the destruction of tortoises and iguanas has been brought under control; though in some cases, control has been achieved only by removing the few remaining individuals on an island and taking them to the station for breeding.

The last 10 tortoises on Espanola (Hood) were brought in for breeding and this has been so successful that nearly 100 of them have been returned to their island home. Research has shown that by the time they are four years old they are big enough so that they are no longer threatened by rats or other predators.

With the land iguanas the breeding program itself has been quite successful, but it has been impossible to return them to their original home. As one scientist said to me, "We'd just be sending back dog food!"

But with all the frustrations, the overall story of the conservation work at the Research Station is one of success—success in being established there to work in the first place, and slow, small steps that sometimes halt and sometimes begin to reverse the ravages of the past.

The latest conservation milestone in the Galapagos story occurred on April 29, 1986. It was then that the government of Ecuador established a Marine Resources Reserve for the Galapagos Islands. This means that all of the internal waters of the archipelago (and a zone that surrounds it for 15 nautical miles out) are now under the same type of protection that the land mass enjoys. This protective move is a well-timed, positive response to the increasing danger of pollution from cruise ships and human settlement. Tourists and residents are exerting greater pressures on fish and crustaceans for food. There is still the unfortunate collection of black coral for sale as souvenir jewelry. Commercial fishing from other countries also must be resisted. It won't always be easy to reconcile the competing interests in these rich waters, but the basic tools are now in place.

All of this complex and often colorful history leads us back to today's visitors and the ecological niche they occupy there. It is my belief that the sheer scientific value of the Islands alone justifies preserving and managing them in the present way. The enormous economic and prestige value of being a UNESCO-designated World Heritage Site and a significant international tourism destination also encourages the local people and the Ecuadorean government to work hard to renew and maintain this precious resource. Access to the Islands is carefully controlled, and if it were not, there would be nothing left for anyone but a few dry rocks with a lot of rats and goats eating themselves into oblivion.

This is not to say that every Islander and every conservationist or visitor is completely satisfied with the way the Park has been set up and managed. But there still is a miracle of conservation taking place—a miracle that all of us, Islanders, scientists and visitors, are supporting by our presence and appreciation. 🐾

Geology and Topography 4

The whole Galapagos archipelago is spread across an area of about 60,000 square kilometers (23,000 square miles). The Galapagos are among the most active volcanic areas in the world, and are of great scientific importance. The land mass of the Islands has resulted from volcanic action which built up the land in one of two ways: layering or uplift.

Most of the islands have the classic conical shape that we associate with volcanic action. Some islands have one dominant cone with small subsidiary cones littering their slopes. (Isabela, for example, has six major volcanic mountains, several of which are active.) These mountainous islands are formed through successive eruptions that build up layer upon layer of lava and ash. This, of course, can happen on already-existent land or under water. If it is the latter, the mountain may eventually reach such size that its peak reaches the surface and it then appears as an island.

By contrast, a few islands, such as Plaza Sur, Baltra and Seymour Norte, were once relatively flat ocean bottom that was raised by shifts of molten material below. This process is called "uplift," and gives these islands the typical "tilted table" look that they have.

The oldest of the Galapagos Islands are in the southeastern edge of the archipelago. Espanola (Hood) has been dated as over 3 million years old. The western islands of Fernandina and Isabela, on the other hand, are less than 700,000 years old.

These islands on the western side of the Galapagos have shown the most recent volcanic activity. There was an eruption of the Fernandina volcano in 1958, obliterating the lake at the bottom of the crater (it re-formed two years later). Then in 1968, the crater floor of Fernandina's volcano suddenly sank another 300 meters below its previous level of 800 meters below the edge of the rim. (The crater itself is 4 by 6.5 kilometers across.) On the day that the floor was subsiding, over 200 earthquakes took place on the island. In 1977 this volcano poured out fresh lava into its crater and then in 1978 it had eruptive activity again.

Isabela also has a very active recent history of volcanic events. In February of 1979 its southernmost volcano, Cerro Azul, erupted over a period of three weeks. Lava was spewed as high as 200 meters into the air. The lava flows are estimated to have reached 10 kilometers in length.

Visitors to the Islands may have a chance to see small-scale volcanic activity if they take the overnight hike up Volcan Alcedo, at the south of Isabela. It has breaks in the inner rim of its crater, out of which steam puffs continuously. This kind of "steam valve" is called a fumarole.

"Hornitos" (little ovens, in Spanish) on Santiago Island

Given their geological history, it is obvious that the topography of the Islands is one of lots of moderately steep slopes, often leading to a major mountain. The height of the Islands ranges from just a few meters above sea level (in the case of those that were uplifted, or are simply very small) to Isabela's Volcan Wolf, which rises 1707 meters (5600 feet) above sea level. Visitors spend most of their time at the low edges of the Islands, but there is usually time for a trip to the Highlands of Santa Cruz, and perhaps for the hike up Volcan Alcedo.

The range of altitudes has great implications for there being an increasing amount of rain at greater heights, for soil development, and for plant and animal life. 🐢

Plant Life

5

Plant life is the basis of all life in the Galapagos, though it is often overshadowed by the animals found there. Yet the plants are often quite beautiful, and they are surely as interesting. They can tell us about their evolutionary processes and the need to preserve them against destructive intruders, such as other plants, grazing and rooting animals, and people.

There is no clear count of the number of plant species in the Islands, but it appears there are about 500 native "higher" plants. About 40 percent of these are endemic to the Islands. There are another 500 species of mosses, liverworts and lichens. Another 200 plant species have been introduced to the Islands, often with very negative results for the native plants. There are a number of native Galapagos plants that are in danger of becoming extinct on the Islands; and in the case of endemic species, totally extinct in the world.

In general terms, it is possible to group the plant life of the Galapagos according to ecological zones which roughly follow the altitude profiles of the Islands. The location of a given spot on an island also plays a role in what type of vegetation is the most characteristic (i.e., at the shore, which might be sandy or rocky or muddy, or further inland).

COASTAL ZONE

The lowest zone is the coastal one, and it can be further divided into wet and dry subdivisions. The wet areas are the mangrove thickets that edge many of the islands. The dry subdivision is the beach and dune areas.

Mangroves have a number of strategies for surviving in a very harsh environment. They are awash with salty water, and they are alternately exposed to wet and dry conditions. The mud in which they anchor themselves is extremely poor in oxygen. They have special means of resisting the salt, of retaining fresh water, of taking oxygen directly from the air, and of spreading their roots very far at the muddy surface rather than going down deep into unstable, low-nutrient earth. They are like watery forests in that they provide a sheltered home for a rich array of wildlife. Shrimp, crabs and small fish find shelter there, and in turn provide food for larger fish, and for the herons, noddies and pelicans that lurk above waiting for a snack.

The dry area of the coastal zone includes the upper beaches themselves, especially those dune areas that are usually above high-tide levels and can support plant life. Plant life here consists of low, spreading plants that are very good at retaining moisture and clinging to what little stable sand or soil that they can. The most striking is the herb *Sesuvium portulacastrum*, which has stems that turn a brilliant rose toward the end of the dry season (roughly October to December). Seeing those mats of color on a gleaming white dune is a memorable experience. You can't miss it on Plaza Sur, or on the path at Sombrero Chino.

ARID LOWLANDS ZONE

The arid lowlands zone stretches inland from an island's beaches up to about 60 meters of elevation. It is best envisioned as a desert, for other than in the very moist years when the El Nino current sweeps down to the Islands, it is indeed a very dry environment. Here plants are scrubby and thorny and sparsely spaced. They, too, have their strategies for retaining moisture and clinging to sandy soil.

This zone is host to some of the more striking cactus plants of the Islands: the candelabra cactus *Jasminocereus thouarsii,* the tree-like prickly pear *Opuntia echios* and the low-lying prickly pear *Opuntia helleri.* On recent lava flows like the one at Sullivan Bay, the short tubes of the lava cactus (*Brachycereus nesioticus*) are scattered here and there.

In this dry area, it is possible to see vines such as the endemic lava morning glory (*Ipomoea habeliana*) and the endemic passion flower (*Passiflora foetida*).

As the land slopes upward the most evident plant is the Palo Santo tree (*Bursera graveolens*). It is silvery grey, and other than often having a rich collection of lichen on its surface, it looks quite dead. There are no leaves much of the time—but when the rare rainy period does come, the leaves burst out, as do its small white flowers. Many of the visitor's walks will lead through swathes of these intriguing trees.

TRANSITION ZONE

As the zone name implies, the transition zone has plants characteristic of both the lower arid zone and the somewhat more moist levels above. In general, the vegetation is more dense and less desert-like in its appearance. There are also greater numbers of species than in the arid zone.

In the category of large shrub or smaller tree type of plant life, there are two common species. One is the pega pega (*Pisonia floribunda*), which is endemic to the Islands. Another endemic species is the guayabillo (*Psidium galapageium*), which occurs in this zone and also farther up in the Scalesia zone. It has white flowers, and a small fruit like the guava, to which it is related.

Less obvious, but equally interesting herbaceous plants of the transi-

Opuntia tree on Plaza Sur ▶

tion zone are the maidenhair fern (*Adiantum concinnum*) and the Galapagos tomato (*Lycopersicon cheesmanii*), which is endemic to the Islands. The latter is quite salt-tolerant, and has been used to develop hybrid tomatoes that can grow in salty soil.

SCALESIA ZONE

This is the first of what are also known as "humid" zones, though it is named after the tree-like plant that most characterizes the levels between 300 and 600 meters. *Scalesia pedunculata*, the "daisy tree," is endemic to the Islands. It is one of the few trees in its family, the asters (order Compositae). It is an example of gigantism in island species. It ranges in height from 5 to 15 meters.

Walking in a Scalesia forest provides an experience rather like walking in the rain forests of the northwest coast of North America. The trees are not as tall, but there are the great beards of moss and coats of lichen on the branches and trunks. There is a sense of stillness, of being surrounded by a rich, dense world that is a home for many kinds of life.

These Scalesia forests have been seriously reduced in numbers and range by human-related activities. Pigs and goats root out the seedlings and feed on older plants. Land was cleared for planting or grazing. Fires occasionally have taken their toll. Plants like the guava (*Psidium guajava*) have infiltrated virtually all of the highlands of the Islands; their dense growth pattern squeezes out most other plants in an area.

The control of goats in some areas has allowed the Scalesia to rebound, but total healing is very far away. The guava is virtually unstoppable once it has been introduced.

MICONIA ZONE

The Miconia zone is the humid zone just above the Scalesia zone, at about 600 to 700 meters elevation. It, too, is named after what once was the dominant plant of this level, *Miconia robinsoniana,* a shrub that grows three to four meters in height. It is very attractive, having regular pointed leaves, with very evident grids of veins forming patterns on the shiny leaves. The leaves are shaded at their edges with yellow or red, which adds to their appeal.

The Miconia is endemic to the Galapagos and is now considered to be the most endangered plant in the Islands. Grazing cattle have been responsible for much of its destruction on San Cristobal and Santa Cruz. You are most likely to go to a Miconia area on Santa Cruz. It is a lovely experience, but you will be able to see how the Miconia has been negatively affected by human activities.

Once you are in the Miconia zone, look on the ground for some of the mosses that grow there. There is a very handsome club moss called *Lycopodium clavatum*. It grows only about 15 centimeters high, but its prickly green stems make it stand out from the surrounding vegetation beneath your feet. The Miconia zone is also the home of the Galapagos cotton (*Gossypium darwinii*). It is endemic to the Islands.

FERN/SEDGE ZONE

The fern/sedge zone occurs at over 900 meters. It is also called the Pampa zone by some scholars. Overall it is the wettest zone of the Islands.

Not all Islands have this elevation and therefore some lack its characteristic vegetation. Also, the amount of rainfall will determine whether the plant life in a given high-elevation location will actually be of this type. Some slopes, protected by a mountain from the prevailing moisture-laden winds, may be too dry to have a fern/sedge zone.

These moist and high conditions are very hospitable to sedges, grasses and ferns. Various mosses and liverworts thrive here as well. No true trees, and few shrubs, grow here. The dominant plant, in the undisturbed state, is the endemic Galapagos tree fern (*Cyathea weatherbyana*). It is quite a shock to see that they are as tall as an adult and that they have fiddleheads as big as a fist. 🌿

Birds

6

Y ou don't have to be a birdwatcher to find the birdlife of the Islands an endless source of enjoyment. And if you are a birdwatcher, you will find yourself in paradise.

It isn't that there is a large number of species in the Islands. There are only 57 resident species, 31 "regular migrants" and 48 species that are classified as "accidentals." But of the 57 resident species, 26 are endemics. The chance to add perhaps 20 of these 26 to your life list is one of the great appeals of the trip for the dedicated birder. And this is not to forget the chance to see a large number of the other resident birds, some of which are rarely seen anywhere else on their range.

For birder and non-birder alike, there is always the opportunity to see the bird life up very close, for extended periods of time. From your boat deck you can watch for hours as the boobies dive for fish. A Hood mockingbird (*Nesomimus macdonaldi*) may land on your hat. You might have to watch your step to avoid tripping over the nest of a flightless cormorant (*Nannopterum harrisi*). Various Darwin's finches will hop in and out of your *panga* (dinghy) or up on the bigger boat to search for tidbits. Off on the horizon a waved albatross (*Diomedea irrorata*) will be skimming the crest of the swells.

Not only is it easy to see many of the bird species found in the Islands, it is often possible to see them busily engaged in nesting activities. The Equator does not have the clearly differentiated seasons experienced in more temperate latitudes. The length of day is constant, and there are no strong light-related cues to set hormones racing and mate searching for mate. Temperatures on the Islands are quite constant, though in El Nino years both air and water temperatures can soar. There are wet and dry seasons, but they are quite ill-defined and not entirely predictable. (And "wet" and "dry" are relative terms, with "wet" often being nearer dry, in terms of measurable precipitation.)

All of these factors put together mean that food supplies may be more evenly spaced out, and some bird species may breed more than once in a year, if the nestlings have gone and there still is enough food to support a new family. There are years when supplies of fish are very low and it is impossible to feed young. There may be other years when the food supplies are very rich. The birds must respond to these circumstances as they arise, and thus there are some species breeding at almost any time of year.

◀ Blue-footed booby and downy chick

Brown pelican and fuzzy-bottomed youngster

Or, in bad years, there may be very few sea birds that come to land and breed successfully.

SEA BIRDS

There are 19 species of sea bird that breed in the Islands, and 3 of these are endemic. The endemic ones are a rather spectacular lot. There is the Galapagos penguin (*Spheniscus mendiculus*), a type of bird we usually associate with the Antarctic and the very tip of South America or the southern shore of Australia. But here under the blast of the equatorial sun we can see this unique species carrying out its everyday life.

The flightless cormorant is endemic, as is the lava gull. The waved albatross is nearly endemic, with a very few pairs nesting on an island near the coast of Ecuador (and their status is very uncertain). The same is true for the swallow-tailed gull (*Creagrus furcatus*), in that only a few pairs nest on an island off the coast of Colombia.

Many of the other sea birds are quite dramatic in their own ways. There are the huge and somehow ominous frigate birds (*Fregata minor* and *F. magnificens*), which are known as "klepto-parasites" because they live off other sea birds by stealing their food. You can often see them harassing a lava gull or booby with a fish in its beak. Suddenly, after an avian dogfight, the smaller bird drops the fish and the frigate bird swoops down to snatch the morsel before it hits the water. It can do this even if it was flying several meters *above* the other bird. If by chance the food hits the water and sinks more than a few centimeters before the frigate bird gets to it, the frigate bird abandons the quest and another chase may soon be on.

Other birds of open water are the masked and blue-footed boobies (*Sula dactylatra* and *S. nebouxii*). The blue-footed is seen very often because it hunts fish in the shallow sea near the shores, where the tour boats spend much of their time. The masked booby fishes much farther out to sea, so they are usually seen at their nests on islands like Daphne Major, Genovesa (Tower) or Espanola.

Many of the sea birds are ground nesters; some of these, like the petrels, nest in burrows. The red-billed tropic bird (*Phaethon aethereus*) nests in the rocky crevices of several islands. The brown noddy nests on cliffs by the sea and in small caves. The blue-footed booby nests on the open ground on a number of the Islands; they are easy to see on Seymour Norte, Daphne and Espanola. Their mating behavior is a charming and amusing sight, as they paddle their bright blue webbed feet up and down, throwing their wings out and head and tail up, wheezing all the while.

But the red-footed booby (*Sula sula*) actually nests in trees and shrubs! They can be seen on Genovesa, peering down on visitors from their rather shaky vantage points. The other shrub- or tree-nesting (it's hard to tell sometimes where a "shrub" leaves off and a "tree" begins in the Islands) birds are both species of frigate bird, and the pelican (*Pelecanus occidentalis*).

LAND BIRDS

Just as the sea birds rely on the sea for their food supply, the land birds rely on the food found on the land masses. In very general terms, the land birds "follow" the vegetation zones of the Islands, because the different plants supply the range of food that is used by different species. However, the division of birds into "sea" and "land" leaves out the birds that spend much of their time on the edges of the land while feeding in the shallows of the sea or in the lagoons, and in the few ponds and lakes of the Islands. These are the flamingo (*Phoenicopterus ruber*); four members of the heron family; and the white-cheeked pintail (*Anas bahamensis*); and two shorebirds, the American oystercatcher (*Haematopus palliatus*) and the common stilt (*Himantopus himantopus*).

Aside from those birds living at the edges of water, there are 28 species of land bird breeding on the Galapagos. Twenty-two of them are endemic, a very large proportion of the whole avian repertoire of the Islands. In types they range from the endemic Galapagos hawk (*Buteo galapagoensis*) to two members of the rail family, which live in the moist, dense highlands of several islands; an endemic dove (*Zenaida galapagoensis*), a cuckoo, two species of owl, two of flycatchers, one warbler, four mockingbirds and the 13 species of the Darwin's finches.

A two-week trip should allow the visitor to see the great majority of the land birds. It will be difficult to locate and identify each of the Darwin's finches, but with a good guide on board and careful attention to the bird guide book, you should be able to see at least half of them. In any case, it will be very clear that they are different in looks and behavior. 🍎

Mammals 7

The mammals of the Galapagos can be grouped according to whether they depend upon the sea or the land for food. One further distinction is that between the native and the introduced species. The latter are more numerous in types and in absolute numbers, and they play a very different role in the Islands than do the native mammals.

MARINE MAMMALS

There are two marine mammals that breed and live much of their life cycles in the Islands. They are both in the eared seal family. One is the sea lion (*Zalophus californianus wollebaeki*), a sub-species of the California sea lion, and the other is the endemic fur seal (*Arctocephalus galapagoensis*).

The sea lion, often seen by visitors, is by far the larger of the two marine mammals here, with the mature males reaching as much as 250 kilograms in weight. The females are appreciably smaller, but still are very sturdy animals. Estimates of the number of sea lions in the Islands vary from 15,000 to 50,000.

The sea lions tend to congregate in groups of females and their pups, with a bull sea lion patrolling the territory that his family group is occupying. These territorial groupings are highly fluid and stay under the sway of a particular male for only two weeks or so.

Younger males who do not have their own territories and collections of mates and young collect in what are called "bachelor groups." As they grow older and more assertive they are able to establish their own relationships with females and set up their own territories. They may do this by "raiding" an existent group when the leading male is off feeding, or squabbling with another male.

Sea lions are very active during the day, especially in the morning and in the late afternoon. They congregate in considerable numbers on sandy beaches, open rocky shores, or areas a few dozen meters inland, but with easy access to the water.

Pups are born most months of the year, except April and May. For the visitor, this means that their chances are very good of seeing young suckling noisily or playing in the waves. When you are swimming, it is not uncommon to have these curious creatures swooshing right next to you.

The Galapagos fur seal is the smallest of the fur seals found in the

◀ **Sea lion basking on Rabida Island beach**

Burros on shore at Urbina Bay—note greenery in El Nino year

southern hemisphere, and it is the only one that lives in tropical waters. Unlike other fur seals, it does not spend most of its time in the water, migrating from one area to another for food or for breeding. These seals spend their lives around the archipelago, with about 30 percent of their time being spent out on land. They have a number of strategies for withstanding the extreme heat and dryness of the arid coastal zone. For example, they spend much of their day in the relative cool of rocky shores and cliffs, where they can get out of the sun. They also feed mostly at night, catching squid and some fish.

There are estimated to be between 30,000 and 40,000 fur seals in the Islands. They breed on most of the Islands, and can be found on all of them. They have their pups between June and December, which tends to be the cooler time of year and the time of the greatest food supply.

Visitors do not see the fur seal nearly as regularly as they do the sea lion; but there are one or two sites, such as the fur seal grottos on Santiago, where there is an excellent opportunity to view them up close.

There are other marine mammals that can be seen in the Galapagos, but they are not land-based for breeding and other activities as are the sea lion and fur seal. These other marine mammals are the whales, dolphins and porpoises that frequent the waters of the archipelago. Most commonly the visitor will see the bottle-nosed dolphin (*Tursiops truncatus*) racing alongside the boat or even riding the bow waves. It is quite possible to photograph them, because they may accompany a boat for many minutes at a time.

Whales, like the humpback and orca (killer whale), are less often seen, but it is by no means impossible for a lucky visitor to spot them.

LAND MAMMALS

Land mammals are not likely to be able to make the long and dangerous trip to far-flung islands; thus it is not surprising that the (surviving) native mammals include two flying ones (bats), and two species of rat.

Rats are among the toughest and most resilient of all animals, and evidently could survive the trip on the mats of vegetable matter that are assumed to have drifted from mainland Ecuador to the Islands. A dense mat of a few square meters would provide them with enough shade, moisture and bits of food to make the trip.

It is thought that there were seven species of rat native to the Islands. However, the devastating impact of the introduced black rat have all but obliterated the native rat. Visitors are not likely to see them—while it is quite common to see the black rat around human habitation.

The two bats are little known and seldom seen.

The introduced mammals have been discussed before in terms of their absolutely negative impact upon the environment of the Islands. Their very different and highly predatory modes of feeding and breeding, and their own extreme caution in the face of humans—when caution is called for—make them a uniformly destructive segment of the mammalian population.

To get some idea of how extensive their presence is, consider the following numbers: between 10,000 and 30,000 cattle on the slopes of Isabela's Volcan Cerro Azul; over 100,000 goats on Santiago; between 500 and 700 burros on Isabela's Volcan Alcedo; 300 to 500 horses running wild on Isabela's Sierra Negra; 200 to 500 dogs on southern Isabela.

There are also thousands of pigs and cats. And, of course, the numbers of rats simply cannot be calculated, though the destructive effects of these smaller mammals on ground-nesting birds and tortoises and iguanas can readily be seen. 🐾

Reptiles

8

T he "totem" animal of the Galapagos is the giant tortoise (*Geochelone elephantopus*, with 11 sub-species, or races, of the original 15 still existent). There is also a sea turtle that occurs widely in the surrounding waters.

The giant tortoises can reach 250 kilograms in weight and measure 150 centimeters across the shell. They look slow and awkward, but in fact they can move quite rapidly and are amazingly flexible in their movements. The most obvious way that a particular race can be distinguished from the others is through the overall size and the shape of the shell, or carapace. The smaller ones (with "saddle backs") are found on Espanola and Pinta, and the largest ("dome-shaped") ones are found on Santa Cruz and Isabela's Volcan Alcedo. The others range between these two ends of the physical spectrum. (Your guide can identify the various races for you.)

The "cousin" of the tortoise, the Pacific green turtle (*Chelonia mydas agassisi*) uses the lagoons of the Islands for breeding; the females lay their eggs in the sand of several Island beaches. This mode of reproduction leaves the turtles very vulnerable to predation. Pigs and rats destroy nests and eat eggs, and hatchlings making their way to the sea are taken by hawks, herons, mockingbirds and frigate birds. Once in the sea, sharks and fish prey upon them. Those that do make it to open water safely, and succeed in living for the next several years, will return to the lagoons and beaches of their origin and reproduce as best they can there. The visitor is most likely to see these turtles during their mating activities at sites like Caleta Tortuga Negra, on Santiago.

The tortoises have suffered terribly from the direct predations of people, from explorers to farmers, who took tortoises in almost unbelieveable numbers.

Tortoises have also suffered from the indirect impact of people: introduced grazing mammals like goats and burros far "out-competed" them for food. And, since tortoises lay their eggs in the ground, the eggs are eaten by cats, pigs and dogs, or trampled by burros. Black rats eat the hatchlings and young turtles are eaten by pigs and dogs.

With all those attacks on their existence, the results are hardly surprising. There were once hundreds of thousands of tortoises on the Islands; there are now less than 15,000. The greatest surviving concentration is the 4000 to 6000 of them in the Highlands of Santa Cruz. It is on

◀ Santa Fe's special land iguana *(C. pallidus)*

Sea turtles mating

walks to these Highlands or at the Darwin Station that the visitor is most likely to be able to see them.

The establishment of the National Park and the combined work of the Park Service and the Charles Darwin Research Station can be credited with saving those races and individuals that remain. At this point 10 of the 11 sub-species are no longer considered to be endangered, though they still are very carefully guarded, reared and returned where possible. The sub-species *abingdoni* has only one living individual, the renowned "Lonesome George." He is being kept at the Research Station, but there is really no hope of finding a female in the zoos of the world and, when George goes, this sub-species will be extinct.

Almost equally well-known as the giant tortoise are the iguanas, marine and land; and much less well-known are the seven species of lizard, the three species of snake, and seven of gecko.

The iguanas of the Islands are very striking both in looks and behavior. They are members of the lizard family. The best-known is the endemic marine iguana (*Amblyrhynchus cristatus*). It is the only truly marine lizard in the world. They average 100 centimeters in length and weigh several kilograms.

They spend much of their time resting in large groups on rocky

Marine iguana on sand, on way to water

shores, soaking up the sun. But when they need to feed, they leave their rocks and swim to nearby patches of seaweed and graze upon them.

They are ground-nesting animals, the female laying eggs in the burrow that she has dug. Unlike the sea turtles, the females stay around their nests for a week or so to guard them from predators. Of course, even with the guarding activity, the nests and the hatchlings are subject to the same sorts of predation as those of the sea turtles.

Though there is just one species of marine iguana, there are seven sub-species. It is possible to see how they differ in size and appearance in some locations. For example, you can see clearly that the iguanas near the fur seal grottos on Santiago are much smaller and more uniformly black than the larger ones of Espanola, which have great splashes of deep red on their sides.

There are two species of land iguana on the Islands (*Conolophus subcristatus* and *C. pallidus*), both of which are endemic. They are quite different in looks and habits from their marine counterparts. They tend to be solitary, while the marine iguanas are highly social and gather in large groups in their resting places. They are much bulkier than the marine iguanas, which are quite sleek by comparison. They are generally yellow, with shading of brown or black on the back ridge. The species *C. pallidus* is found only on Santa Fe; *C. subcristatus* is found on Fernandina (which has the largest population of them), Isabela, Santiago, Santa Cruz, Baltra and Plaza Sur. It is on Plaza Sur that the visitor is most likely to see the latter species, dotting the landscape like huge yellow flowers. They feed on the Portulaca there, and also gnaw through the spiny paddles of the opuntia cactus without any hesitation.

On visits to Santa Fe your guide can usually find some of the individuals of the *C. pallidus* species. But they are few in number, and you are more likely to get a look at them in the breeding pens of the Darwin Station.

The lava lizards of the Islands are often seen by visitors, though it is not easy to distinguish one species from another. They are small (about 30 centimeters), attractive animals, though not very colorful, except for the brilliant splash of orange on the throat of the female. They feed on insects and some plants.

The geckos are not well known and are seldom seen. One obvious reason for this is that they are nocturnal; thus, boat-based visitors would have little opportunity to see them. There are six species, five of them being endemic.

The snakes of the Galapagos—all non-poisonous—are occasionally seen by visitors. About a meter long when fully grown, they feed on lava lizards, marine iguana hatchlings, some bird nestlings and rats. In turn, they are preyed upon by the Galapagos hawk.

A saddle-backed tortoise in pen at the Charles Darwin Research Station

Underwater Life 9

The underwater life of the Galapagos is just beginning to receive attention from scientists and conservationists. Yet it is the largest single habitat in the Islands. It is astonishingly rich and varied, and it very much shapes the quality of all other life in the Islands.

The Galapagos are at the convergence of three major oceanic currents—the north equatorial, the equatorial (Cromwell) and the Humboldt (Peru) coastal current—placing them at the juncture of great underwater rivers that have differing temperatures, lateral and vertical directions, and kinds and amounts of plant, animal and chemical content. All of this adds up to an extremely rich environment that is home to an unimaginable array of underwater life.

The generally cool waters and concomitant dryness of the land are occasionally interupted by the near approach of a current of warm water that usually does not swing down from its ordinary path on the west coast of Central America. When this current, known as El Nino, does dip near the Islands, it causes temporary but drastic changes in the ocean life, in the lives of animals that depend on the ocean for food, and on the weather and everyday life of all the plant and animal inhabitants of the Islands.

Warm water is nutrient-poor water. It holds less oxygen than an equivalent volume of cold water, and with less oxygen there is less underwater plant life (phytoplankton). Less plant life means less food for underwater animal life, from the tiniest crustacean to the biggest shark or whale. Less underwater animal life means less food for seagoing mammals and birds. All of these factors converge during El Nino events.

In El Nino years water temperature soars from its usual 16° to 20°C. to nearly 30°C. The effect on all sea life is dramatic. The change in surface temperatures and weather is also enormous. The Islands are inundated with torrential downpours. Land is washed away. Plants blossom that haven't done so for years. Sea birds may have so little food that they do not even attempt to nest. Sea lions and fur seals may succeed in raising only very few young, if any. By contrast, land birds like the finches may find themselves with so much food that they raise four or five broods over just a few months.

But an El Nino event comes only every seven years or so, and, as devastating as it may seem, it is nothing new to the Islands and most life bounces back very quickly.

Though the marine life of the Islands has been little studied, it does seem clear that it also exhibits the same high proportion of endemic species. Plant life has been estimated to include about 360 species, with 16 percent of these being endemic.

There are an estimated 600 species of molluscs, with 35 percent endemic. There are also 24 species of sea urchin, 28 of sea stars, and 30 species of sea cucumbers.

For the typical visitor, all this underwater life is little seen. The life of the intertidal zone (the areas at the water's edge that appear and disappear with the tides) is very evident, however. The most obvious residents of these wave-splashed areas are the crabs. The Sally Lightfoot (*Grapsus grapsus*) is one of 100 species of crab in the Islands, but its brilliant reds and purples make it the most easily seen. The younger ones are nearly black, but the older ones, which reach the size of a human hand, become a bright orange that really stands out in contrast to the black lava rocks it so often haunts.

In contrast to the striking coloration and substantial size of the Sally Lightfoot crab is the ghost crab (*Ocypode albicans*). Its name comes from its pale, almost translucent coloring, which can make it hard to pick them out as they scuttle along the sand. We saw thousands of them once, on the beautiful beach at the east side of Floreana's Punta Cormoran. They are only a few centimeters in size, but well worth a close-up view—if you can get close enough to one.

To see more sea life, try snorkeling. Snorkeling is easy to do if the water is calm, and even a few minutes can give a very strong sense of the variety and beauty of the marine life. It is also possible to scuba dive in the Islands, by special arrangement with your boat captain before you leave home. (Your travel agent should be able to help you here.)

It will be most interesting to see how the very recent inclusion of the waters of the archipelago within the Park framework will affect both the underwater life itself and the experience of the visitor. There may be increased control on activities like the taking of the delicious langousta, a warm-water "lobster" (actually a crayfish) for visitors' meals, and efforts to increase exposure of the guides and the visitors to the underwater world. Everyone's awareness of its nature and importance will surely be enhanced, and so may their enjoyment of it. 🦀

View up the cliff that has the path to the top on Santa Fe Island ▶

PART II. *Major Islands and Visitor Sites*

Introduction

1

On a typical 10–14 day visit to the Islands, a group will usually be taken to two visitor sites each day. The captain of the boat must operate within the framework of a trip plan which he files with the administrative authorities of the Park and the Ecuadorian navy. Some sites can be visited by all boats, including those which carry the maximum allowable load of 90 people. Some sites, such as Daphne Major, can be visited only once per month, and by boats that have groups of 12 or less. Some sites are always visited because of their accessibility to one of the two airports. Other islands are rarely visited because of their great distance from the "core" of central islands.

Within the framework of the captain's filed trip plan, the speed of the boat, the number of crew and especially the amount of navigational equipment all play a large part in how many sites can be reached. Other factors include the weather, winds, currents, and the captain's estimation of the energy, strength and interest levels of the individual group. Some days more than two places will be visited, and occasionally, most of the day will be spent in transit before a far-flung destination will be reached.

But, given the potential fascination (or discomfort) associated with boat living, it is important to think of that travel time as an active, integral part of experiencing the Islands.

BALTRA

Baltra is not an official visitor site, where the visitor would be told by the naturalist-guide what is special about its flora and fauna. But (at least until late 1986) every person traveling to the Galapagos by air started and finished there. (Now a number disembark and join their boats on San Cristobal, at Puerto Baquerizo Moreno, the capital of the Islands.) At the airport itself, there is a reception center, a waiting area and a canteen. At the receptions kiosks, visitors pay their park entry fees (in U.S. dollars or Ecuadorean sucres—$40.00 U.S. as of 1987) and fill out their entry forms. It is usually a scene of scrambling and confusion, but somehow everything sorts itself out. It is **essential** to keep any papers given out there, usually a thin sheet of paper with your name and a Galapagos stamp on it. Without it—and the equivalent sheet filled out when you enter mainland Ecuador—it is very awkward to leave. There is also a $25 fee to exit the country of Ecuador—be sure to have U.S. funds (cash) in that amount

◀ Fishing for meals

ready for your departure.

As you finish the formalities and wander blinking into the bright sun, there will be a member of your boat crew waiting outside, calling out the name of your boat (which you will already know from your tour operator or travel agent). Buses will provide the brief ride to the harbor where the boats await their passengers.

But even this rather hectic beginning leaves some space for starting to absorb the flavor of the Islands. First, if your flight is approaching the Islands during the garua season (approximately June through December), it is likely that there will be masses of low-lying clouds over the Islands. These are the high-overcast skies that protect you to some degree from the sun, but make photography rather difficult at times. There isn't much rain (except in the times of the El Nino), but these clouds foretell heavy mists and a chill to the air at times, particularly in the evenings. As the Islands show through here and there, they look mostly coppery-brown and gray, and very rugged. Quite regular, conical shapes predominate, from hillocks to mountain-size.

The large number and various sizes of islands usually come as a surprise to visitors. The shorelines gleam white, and the near-shore water is the turquoise blue so often associated with tropical islands. The final approach takes you over Mosquera, a brilliant white sand-spit that you may be able to visit later.

As you stand around waiting, look a little farther to the scrub areas nearby. You are sure to see the first Darwin's finches of the trip scrabbling around on the ground. A couple of different beak sizes will be evident, and so will be the browns of the females and the blacks of the males. There won't be time here for much more than a glance, but when you reach the boats you will experience your first acquaintance with two continuously interesting and important parts of the trip—the food and the blue-footed boobies.

The cook on any boat rapidly assumes great importance, in my experience, and maintains it for the rest of the trip. Passengers select their quarters, start putting away their gear, and then come up for food and sun. There's usually an excellent lunch of soup, bread, fish, a salad of fresh vegetables or fruit and cold drinks. The cost of the food is included in the whole trip fare; but after the first free drink, a running tab is kept of each person's consumption of beverages. (You pay up on the last day. Both pop and beer are inexpensive.) This is the time to take your seasick pills (although it is best to have started the morning before leaving the mainland, and then take another one on the boat), and then to go out on the deck and watch the boobies.

In this harbor, as in virtually all sheltered water, boobies are busy fishing or standing basking on rocks. The first sight of a booby's wheeling plunge into the aquamarine sea seems to signal that your Island adventure has really begun. Pelicans may join the boobies in their hunt, and lava gulls often will come to sit on the panga, which is tied to the larger boat. Even a

Getting ready for the day, after sleeping out all night

sea lion may hop up into the panga, just a few meters away. Everyone calls everyone else over to come and look, but the sea lion is generally oblivious to the attention. 🐚

Santa Cruz and Nearby Sites

2

S anta Cruz is located near the center of the whole Galapagos archipelago. Because Baltra Island is very near and many visitors land at the airport there, Santa Cruz and the islands nearby are often the first series of sites visitors see. Puerto Ayora, the main settlement on Santa Cruz, is also the home of the Galapagos National Park administration and the Charles Darwin Research Station. You'll enjoy a visit to Puerto Ayora, and your itinerary will probably include side trips into the moist Highlands of the island.

There are a number of small islands easily reached from Santa Cruz, including tiny Plaza Sur, and Mosquera with its glaring white beach and warm protected waters — great for swimming. Not far from Santa Cruz to the south is Santa Fe. It has one of the most appealing coves for anchorage and a good swim in calm water. Santa Fe also offers a great chance to see the giant cactus trees up close, and with luck you'll see some of the land iguanas that are found only there.

Santa Cruz (Indefatigable)

S anta Cruz is really the hub of the Islands for the visitor. It is centrally located in relation to the other islands, has many visitor sites and is the home of the Charles Darwin Research Station and the headquarters of the Galapagos National Park. It also is the most "developed" village in the islands, in terms of amenities for the visitor. Your group may stay overnight in a small hotel there, you can eat in one of several modest restaurants, and there are a few stores where you can do some tourist-style shopping (T-shirts, post cards, etc.).

PLAYA LAS BACHAS

Playa Las Bachas is often the first stop for all boats that have taken on passengers from the Baltra airport. The ride is only an hour or so from the first harbor, so Las Bachas is reached in mid- to late afternoon. It is a "wet" landing, where the panga pulls into shallow water or right up on ground and then everyone hops out. It's best to carry your lightweight walking shoes, and disembark barefoot. The beach is sandy, and since the cove is sheltered, the water is rarely rough, so it's altogether an easy landing.

◀ Great blue heron

SANTA CRUZ ISLAND

1. Road to airport
2. Playa Las Bachas
3. Caleta Tortuga
4. Pit craters
5. Cerro Crocker
6. Media Luna
7. Agricultural Zone
8. Tortoise Reserve
9. Tortuga Bay
10. Lava tube

Las Bachas is a sudden immersion into one of the most typical Galapagos shoreline environments. First, there is the beach—in this case with white sand, while others may have red or black. This beach is a major egg-laying site for sea turtles. The name, Las Bachas, refers to the indentations left in the sand by laying turtles or departing hatchlings.

Where the beach rises to a low crest, there is a band of tangled bushes — saltbush (*Cryptocarpus pyriformis*) and even the prickly pear cactus (*Opuntia helleri*). Next you approach a slight depression which holds brackish water.

On the shore and in the bushes, you will almost certainly see your first marine iguanas. They sit quietly, occasionally doing "push-ups" in place if they become a little agitated. It's easy to take pictures, though you should take care to compensate for the blackness of the iguana's skin in comparison with the glaring white sand.

Flamingos at Playa Las Bachas, in an El Nino year

The harbor at Puerto Ayora on a drizzly morning

I once took some good pictures, very close, of a lone marine iguana. What I managed to disguise by the close-up was the fact that it was nearly a crowd scene. Six other people ringed the iguana and four different languages were being spoken as we all clicked away.

Past the beach, at the lagoon, there is a good chance that there will be a couple of species of shorebird (common stilt, *Himantopus himantopus*, or wandering tattler, *Heteroscelus incanum*) and—most impressive—flamingos (*Phoenicopterus ruber*). In the bird guide to the Galapagos it points out that the flamingos are some of the shyest of Island birds and that every effort should be made not to disturb them in any way. Usually at Las Bachas it is possible to hang back a bit at the edge of the bushes and acquire a little camouflage in that way. You will notice that your guide will be speaking in a low voice to minimize disturbance and to set an example for others.

On your return to the beach area itself some of the group may want to do a little snorkeling; it is a nice quiet place to try this. Ask your guide beforehand if there will be time.

Your return to the panga will mark the first time for a most important Galapagos ritual: foot cleaning. It is imperative that you wash off any sand, seeds, or other debris from your feet and shoes. This is to prevent the artificial transport of plant life from one island to another, and to help keep the boat clean. Sand can pile up very quickly and become an irritant on a well-populated boat.

PUERTO AYORA, SANTA CRUZ ISLAND

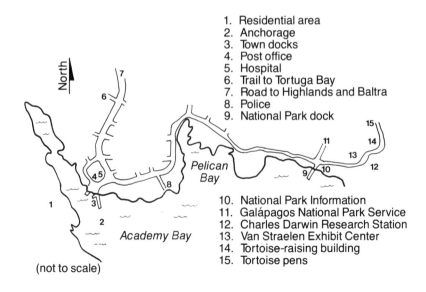

1. Residential area
2. Anchorage
3. Town docks
4. Post office
5. Hospital
6. Trail to Tortuga Bay
7. Road to Highlands and Baltra
8. Police
9. National Park dock

10. National Park Information
11. Galápagos National Park Service
12. Charles Darwin Research Station
13. Van Straelen Exhibit Center
14. Tortoise-raising building
15. Tortoise pens

(not to scale)

PUERTO AYORA

The town of Puerto Ayora is the one settlement that is usually visited by all tourists. It is also the supply center for the boats, which must come in here between trips or halfway through very lengthy trips to replenish any necessary supplies. Some trip plans include just a short day (or even less) in town, visiting the Darwin Station and perhaps taking a ride into the interior to visit a farm, or to walk through the lava tubes, or in the Tortoise Reserve. In either case, the stay is too short to get any more than the most superficial idea of how the 3000 or so local residents carry out their daily lives.

There are several small stores in town, a few snack bars, a bank, medical facility, school, churches, and a small navy emplacement. Puerto Ayora is of particular interest to the conservation-oriented visitor because the headquarters of both the Darwin Station and the Galapagos National Park are located there.

A post office just at the landing, past the Ninfa restaurant, is *the* place to mail your postcards and letters. (All mine mailed from here made it to their destinations.) Virtually all of the stores or restaurants have postcards and many of the small businesses carry really attractive Galapagos T-shirts. They are far above the quality of the usual tourist T-shirt designs and are reasonably priced.

If you've discovered you want something special to eat on the boat (it was more hot chocolate on one of my trips), or you need another tape cassette, it will be easy to accomplish in Puerto Ayora. The people are very friendly and helpful and do not seem to be suffering from burn-out as hosts to tourists.

CHARLES DARWIN RESEARCH STATION

The Station is an easy 30- to 45-minute walk from the main boat landing, or you may be taken by panga to the Station's own dock. The walking route is along one of the two principal roads through the town; a comfortable walk on packed dirt/gravel, with interesting ongoing town life to see. There might be time after your visit to the Station to have a cool drink at one of the hotels, little restaurants or snack bars along the way.

As you enter the grounds of the Station there is a small building on the right that serves as an information center and a shop. It is run by the National Park Service, and sells postcards, posters, books and other Galapagos and Darwin Station memorabilia.

Then you move along to the main buildings. As you go through this small "compound," with its exhibit buildings and the low outlying laboratory facilities, you may be struck with how modest the whole setup is. All of the important research, carried on by an array of international scientists, and all the training of park natrualists and liaison work between the National Park and the Darwin Research Station is done on a very small budget, with

Young tortoises in outdoor rearing pens

relatively few people. So, as pleasant as the surroundings are, they are not impressive in themselves—it's the results of the work of the occupants that achieves world-wide attention and approval.

The first building within the compound is the Van Straelen Exhibit Hall. It houses informative displays that explain the geological history of the Islands. The next stop is the tortoise exhibit building. It contains displays explaining the evolution of the tortoises on the Islands. It also has actual rearing pens for these intriguing beasts. (There are also restrooms right next to this building.)

The building is circular and its perimeter is divided into wedge-like segments. The inner wall has glass sections to protect the tortoises from too-curious visitors. Each segment contains a group of very young tortoises from one of the islands (or part of islands) where distinct races of tortoises live. Or rather, where they are nearly extinct or are having great difficulty surviving because of the predations of introduced species.

In the case of the Hood Island tortoises, adults actually are being bred at the station. The entire adult population of these tortoises was taken from that island in the late 1960s because their situation was so precarious; now they are bred here and kept until predators on Hood can be sufficiently reduced to allow some tortoises to be returned safely.

For the other races of tortoise, eggs have been brought in, incubated and hatched, and some of each race are there on display. (There are larger numbers being raised in pens beyond the areas that are accessible to the public.) The tortoises in the display hall are from one to five years old; a typical five-year-old measures about 30 centimeters across. Their carapaces have numbers on them to help keep track of their progress. After five years, a tortoise is usually big enough to withstand attack back on its home ground — *if* there is enough food left after the goats and other grazing animals have taken their toll. As with many of the iguanas being raised for conservation purposes, some tortoises cannot be returned to their original homes until ways are found of reducing or eradicating the threats to their survival.

The next area that can be visited is an open compound which contains huge adult tortoises, in several different enclosures. Visitors can enter the largest enclosure and walk right up to the tortoises as they feed and sleep and drink from the artificial pond. It is a great place for photographing. Yet, with all the people there, it is still possible to observe very closely how the tortoises move and feed (*how* do they avoid the cactus spines when they chew?) and even doze with head resting on outstretched foot.

Also, the very artificiality of the displays and pens and compounds somehow brings closer the uniqueness of the Islands in their natural state. It is quite moving to see even a small portion of the work that has to go into trying — in some cases successfully — to save these tortoises and land iguanas before it is too late for them all, though it has been too late for some.

The Station grounds are also interesting for the great diversity of plant and animal life there. Several species of finch can be observed at leisure, lava herons fish near the dock, lava lizards abound and marine iguanas are often seen in the low-lying mangrove areas near the entrance.

Looking at the exhibits in the Tortoise Raising Hall

THE HIGHLANDS

Much of the visiting from island to island is to places very near sea level, so there are not many opportunities to experience the more moist and lush habitat of those islands which have elevations from 900 to 1500 meters, or more. Santa Cruz is the most likely place to go, both because of its central location and because of its fully developed vegetation zones, which are accessible by motor vehicle.

Most of the tours now include a trip to the Highlands as a regular part of their itinerary. The jumping-off points for the trails into interesting Highland areas — the pit craters called Los Gemelos, the lava tubes on private property that can be visited for a very small fee, the crater called Media Luna or the Tortoise Reserve itself—are anywhere from 30 minutes to more than an hour (by car) from Puerto Ayora. The hikes can last from a few minutes to several hours.

If you are one of the few visitors who are not part of a tour, there are buses to the Highlands, but they do not operate on a recognizable schedule. However, by asking around, you can find out how to take one of the local buses to the trailheads. Just be sure, if you are staying for a few days on your own, that **both hotel and return air trip are absolutely confirmed.** I did this once at the end of the group segment of my visit and it was very satisfactory. The tour guide helped with the hotel arrangements and flight confirmations.

There is a modest range of hotel facilities in the town. A little shopping around should turn up something in your price and comfort range. Meals are available at some of the hotels and several small restaurants are tolerable. Just peer in, see what others are eating, and talk to the manager, who'll probably be there. Spanish and English are the most likely languages to be used. Cheese, bread and fruit are generally available at the local market and in stores. Recently a little "supermarket" appeared on the main street, with a reasonable selection of fresh and canned goods.

TORTOISE RESERVE

Visiting the Tortoise Reserve can be quite a trek, but it's worth the effort. The Reserve is an "unregulated" area, which means that it's not necessary to have a licensed guide accompanying visitors. Of course, the same Park rules about not disturbing plant or animal life apply as always, and most visitors are with their guide anyway.

To get there, you have to get to the tiny settlement of Santa Rosa, on the road that runs completely across the island. The trail begins there. The ride takes about half an hour. If you are not with a guided group, be sure to tell the driver what your destination is. The other passengers will tell you when you've arrived (it's not always easy to tell what is a settlement and what is just a collection of houses). They will also tell you where the trail picks up, just behind a few fields and buildings to the left of the road, as you are heading away from Puerto Ayora.

Boat building—on the road to the Research Station

Tortoises rambling in the reserve

Large-billed flycatcher

The walk to the Reserve is at first gently rolling, then gradually descends. The path is very easy to follow. There are several things to notice along the way. One is the vegetation, which is typical of the rich, humid Scalesia zone. It is evident that the trees are much more leafy than the spare Palo Santo that is seen in the dryer, lower areas. Their bark is covered with lichen and tufts of moss. Look for the long, regular and colorful leaves of the Miconia bushes and the thin umbrella shapes of the Scalesia trees.

As you approach the fencing for the Reserve boundary, see how strikingly different the agricultural land is from the relatively undisturbed Reserve lands. On one side of the trail is the agricultural land, which has banana or papaya plantations, or has been cleared in places for cattle pasturage. On the other side of the trail is the richness of land left somewhat on its own. Seeing these contrasts can help the visitor understand how dramatic an effect human settlement can have on a fragile place like this. It also points out the close relationship between competing claims for land use in the Islands.

Bird-watching is excellent in this area. Both the large-billed and vermilion flycatchers can be seen. It is often overcast and shady along the trail and that can make photography frustrating, but a fast film will reap rewards. (It was always a mystery to me why the vermilion flycatchers seemed to spend most of their time on the lowest branch of the most shady tree — when they were near enough to photograph, anyway.)

But there were really special opportunities for once-in-a-lifetime shots, such as the vermilion flycatcher framed by wisps of grey moss, and another one sitting on the great domed back of a tortoise, snapping up the insects that the tortoise stirred up.

Short-eared owls may be seen here, though I missed them. And the bird guidebook says that in rainy periods there are a number of short-lived ponds where the white-cheeked pintail and both species of rail can be seen.

But it's the tortoises that put the capstone on this walk. Even before reaching the actual Reserve boundaries, you are likely to start coming across the giant, dome-backed tortoise characteristic of Santa Cruz. It seems that they like to stick to the paths as much as the humans do, especially if it's muddy!

Seeing these beasts is unforgettable. On one trip, I looked for them eagerly; suddenly, there was a tortoise, and then another in a few minutes. They were a little taller than the bushes and I'd first see just the top of their backs. And as I got closer they'd make a hissing noise. They would pull in their head and feet and as they did this there would be the sound of air being pressed out — like a bellows — a puffing sound with little whistling overtones. Even when they shifted their head as they fed, this puff would happen! It's really a very soft and pleasant sound.

The chances of sighting tortoises may vary some by the season, with encounters more likely in the more moist and cool times (roughly June–December). But if you take along some water and snacks (leaving no trash behind!), walk slowly, and give yourself a good two hours each way for a leisurely walk, luck may be with you.

Also, to assure a comfortable trip, bring a light rain jacket (the kind that folds into its own pocket is ideal) or windbreaker, because it can get fairly damp and a little chilly at these elevations. Lightweight slacks or heavier walking shorts should be adequate, and sturdy shoes that you don't mind getting damp and filthy are also a good idea.

Once back at the road, be prepared to wait for the local bus. When I was there, there was a very informal "cantina" which seemed to be operated by the bus driver or some associate of his. The cold drinks were very welcome after the sticky, humid hike. We weren't allowed to pay. A mainland Ecuadorian who had been hiking the same trail with friends insisted—as happened several other times in similar circumstances—that we be his guests, so we would "remember that Ecuador was a good place." No problem there.

MEDIA LUNA

The trip to Media Luna, a half-moon-shaped volcanic cinder cone, is less strenuous than the Tortoise Reserve hike. It is about an hour each way, along an easy-to-follow, gently ascending path. This too is an unregulated zone, within Park boundaries. It is possible to walk freely, following your inclination and those paths or trails that are clear. Heavy mists are common, so attention must be paid to landmarks for finding your way back. A rain jacket is a definite asset also.

To get to Media Luna it is necessary to have transport to the settlement of Bella Vista. (It's only 7 kilometers from town, but you're better off saving your energy and time for the trail itself.) As for the Tortoise Reserve, if you are on your own, ask people where the trail begins (to the right, behind the school playground). It is quite clear once you get going.

First the trail passes through the agricultural zone, and there are avocado and papaya groves, with wild guava bushes in abundance. As you continue up the gentle slope, the walk offers much the same scenery as the early part of the Tortoise Reserve hike; there are the Scalesia and Miconia plants and also the grassy "pampa" (fern/sedge) zone vegetation. There is a particularly good opportunity to see the giant ferns there. They tower overhead and it is almost eerie to look *up* to a fern and see that its delicate "fiddlehead" is so large.

The bird-watching is good along the path, with a likelihood of seeing the woodpecker and large tree finches. The birding guide book says that at the higher levels, the upper limit of the Miconia zone, the Galapagos rail can be heard and that a little lower down the paint-billed crake (*Neocrex erythrops*) can be found. Hawaiian petrels (*Pterodroma phaeopygia*) also nest in this area, but are severely hampered in their nesting success by the predations of feral animals. Efforts are being made to assess the situation and make some improvements, but it is a most dispiriting task.

On clear days, a visit to the Media Luna location is very rewarding; the view extends all the way down the sloping side of Santa Cruz to Puerto Ayora. After a number of days on a boat, going from one arid place to another, usually spending most time at sea level, this sweep of lush forest, grassland, and the turquoise harbor of the port is most refreshing.

LAVA TUBES

Even though these tubes are not an official park visitation site, they are certainly distinctive and interesting. Again, arrangements will have to be made by the guide, or independently, in order to reach the location, which is off a side road from Bella Vista. There is a modest home near the beginning of the path and someone comes out to collect a very small entrance fee.

In the tube — note collapsed ceiling ▶

After a brief walk, you will encounter a big hole in the ground which forms a tunnel stretching beyond sight below and forward. The actual descent into the tube is just a scramble down some rather large rocks. A steadying hand from a friend will probably be all the help necessary. Then after a few meters' walk the light begins to disappear, so a flashlight is quite important.

The lava tubes were formed by rushing rivers of lava. Their outer surface cooled more quickly than the contents in the interior of the flowing mass, so the outer surface hardened sooner. The inner part could continue to flow until it, in effect, emptied itself onto the earth; thus, a hollow tube was left behind. There are actually two tubes here, the first curving down and then up to surface level. After a few meters on the surface you descend again into the second tube. One of the tubes has had a cave-in of a part of its roof and the hole, a couple of meters in diameter, admits light. The other tube is quite thoroughly dark. Even with these dim conditions, flashlight or not, walking in the tubes is quite easy. There's just the occasional rock or boulder to go over or around.

The tubes are about the length of several buses, and about three stories (10–15 meters) high. The walls are scored by the lava flow, but are otherwise quite straight and smooth. At the end of the last tube there is a makeshift handrail to help visitors negotiate the final slope up. When I was there, the exit was lovely as the light filtered back into the tube entrance, illuminating the greenery at the surface and highlighting the ferns that were able to grow part way down into the tunnel itself.

LOS GEMELOS

Los Gemelos ("the twins") are two pit craters, sections of the earth's surface that have fallen in on themselves as a result of movements of the earth's crust. At one time there was a layer of lava at the surface; when volcanic action below opened up an underground "bubble," the surface collapsed onto itself, creating several acres of pit craters. Over time, vegetation has clothed the slopes of these depressions and the visitor sees a rich bowl of greenery.

Los Gemelos are located on either side of the road that goes between Puerto Ayora and Baltra, just 11 kilometers out of the port. It is a common destination for groups on their day in town. The site is an attractive one, just a few minutes' walk into the open area, which is in the Scalesia forest zone and is rich in bird and plant life. The large-billed and vermilion flycatchers may be seen, and if you're lucky a short-eared owl may be perched on one of the moss-encrusted Scalesia branches.

CALETA TORTUGA NEGRA

This is "black turtle cove," a tidal lagoon that is almost maze-like in its complex shape. It is etched into the north coast of Santa Cruz, just

Immature yellow-crowned night heron in mangrove

southwest of Baltra. The cove has a narrow entrance, reached after a brief panga-ride, and then it stretches nearly a kilometer inland and at its farthest end is over half a kilometer wide. You will stay in your panga the whole time; after you have motored into the lagoon, your guide will cut the motor and just paddle quietly so that you can get the most out of the visit.

The entrance into the lagoon is a very good place to see all three kinds of mangrove plant: the red (*Rhizophora mangle*), white (*Laguncularia racemosa*) and black (*Avicennia germinans*). Your guide will tell you how to distinguish one from the other.

Here, too, you can see very clearly the role that mangroves play in providing habitat for a wide variety of wildlife. Oysters cling to the roots, pelicans perch on their heights, herons pick their way along the prop-roots that link the branches to the muddy bottom. Mullet flash in and out of the finger-like roots underwater.

Once you are well into the lagoon you are likely to be in for some very exciting moments. The brackish, calm waters are frequented by the white-tipped shark and rays of the spotted eagle and mustard (or "golden") varieties. Each time I have been there there have been a number of the sharks, just sliding below the boat, or gathering in the shadow of the overhanging mangrove branches.

The rays are also an intriguing feature. The spotted eagle rays are easily a meter wide. They seem to hover at the surface and even raise their "heads" right up out of the water now and then.

The mustard rays are smaller and when I saw them they were traveling in groups. They are very graceful, with the smooth movement of their "wings," showing alternately the cream-colored underside and the dull mustard color of their backs. They are diamond-shaped, and they were traveling in diamond-shaped formation. The pattern-within-a-pattern of their movement was quite lovely.

There is a real possibility that you will see the green Pacific marine turtle here, for they gather here to mate. On one of my trips we were sitting quietly in the panga, when suddenly we heard a puff, a gentle moist exhalation behind us. We turned and saw the beak of a turtle just rising from the surface of the water. Then there was another puff a few meters in the other direction, then another and another. Next we noticed the water being roiled not far away. We went a bit closer, and sure enough, the back of a turtle showed, then a flipper appeared, then the paler belly and another side and back. It became obvious that this was a pair of turtles locked into a copulatory embrace. They do this for hours, gently rolling, sometimes entirely submerged, sometimes both heads appearing as they come up for air. submerged, sometimes both heads appearing as they come up for air.

I found it interesting that the experience of this lagoon obviously brought our group of very diverse people very close to each other. There was a sense of peaceful, smiling affection that permeated the panga as we returned to our home boat, and which was sustained throughout the remainder of the trip. Not what we had come to the Islands for, but definitely an enjoyable result of the trip just the same.

Other Islands: Plaza Sur, Santa Fe, Mosquera, Daphne Major, Seymour Norte

PLAZA SUR

Plaza Sur is a small island, the southern of a pair of somewhat crescent-shaped islands not far off the east side of Santa Cruz. Plaza Sur is only 130 meters wide, and a kilometer long. Unlike the conical volcanic islands, it is the result of shifts in the earth's crust, which have lifted it above the surface of the water. It is like a tilted table top, rising gradually from the beach to cliffs of about 20 meters on the south side.

Landing on the islands is usually easy, because there is a small cement jetty which the panga can pull up to. If the water is calm, you should be able to make a dry, though sometimes slippery, landing and then take the easy walk of about one hour. The only obstacle to landing (a temporary one) is that some of the numerous sea lions also love to lie on the jetty. So the guide usually has to clap or otherwise make noises to make the original occupants depart, usually rather grumpily.

Once on the island, the first thing you'll notice is the vegetation. This is one of the islands with tree-sized opuntia, or prickly pear cactus (*Opuntia echios*). They are very handsome with their bright russet bark, textured in a mosaic of elongated diamond-shaped plates. Rising from the bark are veritable explosions of gray spines, well over three centimeters in length. Along the "branches" and at their tips are great flashy paddles. These green paddles are a source of food for the finches and the land iguanas (*Conolophus subcristatus*) that are common here. It is quite wonderful to see the sturdy, pink-tongued iguanas stand on their hind legs to munch on those spine-laden pads. How they don't get punctured is a mystery!

I have been to Plaza Sur in an El Nino year, when the vegetation was at least knee-high and very green. The portulaca (*Portulaca oleracea*) was in splendid bloom, with the yellow flowers matching the brightest hues on the land iguanas, which, from a distance, stood out from the greenery like overgrown flowers themselves.

But the more typical condition of extreme dryness prevails most years, and there are swathes of grey, root-like vegetation matted across the ground. In great contrast to the drab background there is the brilliant rose-red of the *Sesuvium* plant, a colonizer of harsh sandy zones near the water. There are two species, *S. portulacastrum* and *S. edmonstonei*, which is endemic to the Islands.

The Sesuvium has "branches" with a fleshy quality as many arid-zone plants do. That is, they are a "succulent," and like cacti can hoard moisture in their fleshy parts, which are covered by a waxy exterior that retards moisture loss.

The path circles the eastern half of the island. It is a classic example of park trail design, unobtrusively marked by the little gnarled posts of local wood, painted with a band of white and black. The trail is easy to follow and it goes exactly where you would want to go. First, it crosses the island, and up a gradual incline. The sea lions are left behind and the light yellow and gray-green land iguanas begin to appear more frequently.

Soon the path comes closer to the black rocky cliffs. Sheer in places, crumbly in others — do exercise caution here — the cliff edge is a great place for bird- and sea-watching. Swallowtail gulls (*Creagrus furcatus*) are usually there, mottled gray and white young dotted along the cliffside, and the adults wheeling and swooping in the incessant wind. (A windbreaker is a useful item here.) As they land against the air currents there is usually a good opportunity to photograph them, wings outstretched, forked tail spread.

Not landing, but often very much in evidence, are the red-billed tropic birds (*Phaethon aethereus*) circling the island. There will be blue-footed and masked boobies, some perched on the cliff face. Hundreds of Audubon's shearwaters (*Puffinus lherminieri*) may be swirling over the water's surface below. Frigate birds are ever-present.

The cliff edge is a good place for spotting sea-life as well. Two out of my three visits we spotted manta rays, "as big as a coffee table," cruising sail-like just under the surface of the water. Once a hammerhead shark gave us a thrill, cruising below. There were also shoals of mullet devouring the same plankton the mantas feed on.

On the final quarter of the walk the trail traces the lower side of the island. First, near the water, are some small sandy areas lined with rocks. Marine iguanas bask and bob their heads in the sun. Continuing on, there is even less vegetation and lots of rocks and boulders to pick your way through. The rocks have a shiny white patina, the result of year after year of sea lion bodies polishing their own excrement as they lumber over their territory to and from the water.

Plaza Sur is one of the few islands which have largely been spared the ravages of introduced species or uncontrolled human use. Other than goats there have been no introduced animal species, and the goats were eliminated by 1961. It is a good way to see what an island can be like: dense with wildlife, its natural plants intact, its spare beauty surrounding the visitor and the inhabitants alike. However, the heavy visitor use is taking its toll, and Plaza Sur may be taken off the list of sites that can be visited by the large cruise ships, or some other limitations of numbers of visitors may be put in place.

SANTA FE

Part of the visit to Santa Fe includes one of the few fairly rigorous segments of trail at the frequently visited sites. But it also has one of the most sheltered and beautiful anchorages of all the ones you will stay in. This deeply indented cove is marvelous for a quiet rest and swim after the slog up the cliff to see the species of land iguana (*Conolophus pallidus*) that is unique to this one island.

Santa Fe is about a three-hour boat ride from the southeast edge of Santa Cruz. It is another one of the uplifted islands, like Plaza Sur, Baltra and Seymour Norte. It does have the traces of surface volcanic activity, however; there are remains of underwater lava flows that were uplifted as the whole island plate was pushed to the surface.

After a wet landing on a small sandy beach, the group will probably be taken up to the top of a distant cliff. You will be looking for the land iguanas, which tend to frequent certain areas. Your guide will point these out.

The trail ascends gently at first, but at the base of the cliff there is

---

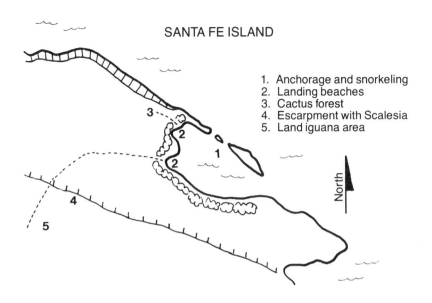

SANTA FE ISLAND

1. Anchorage and snorkeling
2. Landing beaches
3. Cactus forest
4. Escarpment with Scalesia
5. Land iguana area

North

perhaps five minutes' worth of steep ascent. The path is clear—there's nowhere else to go — but it can be crumbly and a little wearing if the temperature is already high. A helping hand from the guide or other visitors is really all that's needed to reach the top.

On the way up, notice the huge opuntia trees here, and the Scalesia plants at the upper levels. Though Scalesia is associated most often with the moist uplands, there are in fact 14 species of it, several of which occupy the arid coastal zones. (The species you see here is *Scalesia helleri*.) You may notice that some of the plants on the steep slope have been tagged so that scientists can trace their development.

The trek to the top of the escarpment isn't always rewarded with a sighting of the iguanas, but it is pretty common to see them there. This species is distinguished by its unusually heavy ridge of spikes along its backbone, rather like extremely tough, pointed fingernails. They can move briskly, though those I saw were deeply attached to the warm earth and the only movements evident were light breathing and the occasional eye blink.

Once you've made the trek to the escarpment, there may be time to take the short, low trail in the opposite direction. It goes to a very fine stand of opuntia trees (*Opuntia echios*). The brief walk is made more interesting by having to side-step the usual group of sea lions that are lolling on the beach and in the shade of nearby rocks.

After you return to your boat, you will have a chance to enjoy the other highlight of Santa Fe — its beautiful cove. There is a long arm of rocks stretching from the beach and ending in a small island. You will be situated about halfway along the arm, enfolded by it. First check out the island itself for Galapagos hawks. They are regulars here. Once at night we were visited by an owl, which landed momentarily in our rigging. Pelicans are likely to be hovering around and frigate birds will be attracted by the boat.

But this is a place to be at one with the water. In such a protected cove, swimming is easy and snorkeling is good all along the inside of the rocky arm. You'll be joined by sea lions and other creatures as well.

Santa Fe is another island that was once plagued by goats, but they were eradicated in 1971. Thus what the visitor sees is an island well on its way to recovery. It's good to know that such beauty and distinctiveness has a real chance to continue on its natural course.

MOSQUERA

Mosquera is a playground of sand, rocks and tide pools. Sea lions join the visitors, lolling around, sunning and swimming.

The best view of Mosquera comes just as the plane is turning for its final descent to the Baltra runway. Look for the gleaming curve of white sand — that's Mosquera flashing below you.

The panga takes visitors to the sandy beach for a wet landing. There is a shallow cove, quite well protected from the open sea. Somehow the water in that cove seemed warmer than elsewhere. The snorkeling is easy and very interesting near the small points of rock that emerge from the sea bed in several places.

But the land turns out to be unexpectedly exciting. First, the whole island is a free zone, where you can wander at will. Though the island is tiny, this freedom gives you a great sense of space. Then there are the tide pools calling out for exploration. You quickly see that you have to watch out not to get too close to the numerous sea lions loafing in the shallow water. Sally Lightfoot crabs (*Grapsus grapsus*) abound, and the pools are rich with other animal and plant life that live in this intertidal zone.

Bird-watching is good, too. Pelicans and boobies post themselves on the higher rocks, shorebirds peck and probe at the water's edge. I saw three semi-palmated plovers (*Charadrius semipalmatus*) and a sanderling (*Crocethia alba*) — two old friends from the North.

If you have time, just plop down on the sand and make like a sea lion yourself. The heat and glare from the sand is moderated by the breeze. You may see the daily plane hurtling over you, and you'll feel lucky to be where you are, well into the trip and already acquiring a luscious tan.

DAPHNE MAJOR

A visit to Daphne Major is an infrequent privilege. Each captain is allowed to take a group of 12 or less there just once a month, with the permission of the Darwin Station and the Park Superintendent. Check with

Daphne Major from a distance. Note the trail from the lower left side up to the rim.

your captain as to whether your group may visit this tiny island.

A small volcanic cone rising abruptly out of the sea just north of Santa Cruz and west of Baltra, it is a frequently seen landmark. But its fragility, and value to basic research on its varied bird life, has caused it to be set aside by the Park largely for the use of scientists. (There is a Daphne Minor. It is a much smaller "sibling" of Daphne Major, just 6 kilometers north of it. Daphne Minor is only .08 square kilometers in area, four times smaller than Daphne Major.)

Daphne Major is slightly oval in shape, but from almost any direction at sea level it looks like a completely circular cone that has been lopped off crisply at the top. The landing is on its south side. Some consider the athletic leap and scramble from boat to land as one of the most difficult landings on the trip. Once on land, there are a few rocks to surmount and then a narrow, smooth path that winds gently upward to the crater rim, a walk of about 350 meters, one way.

This is another one of those walks where you have to watch your step, because the path is often occupied by nesting blue-footed boobies. (It's their home, after all.) If you look at the rocky outcroppings, the scattered clusters of boulders, you are likely to see the masked booby at its nest. This is a wonderful chance to make comparisons between the female and male blue-footed boobies. The females look like they have a much larger pupil in their eye, a dark center surrounded by a relatively thin ring of gold. Conversely, the males have a very small dark center in their eyes. (It is not a difference in pupil size, actually, but a difference in the degree that the dark coloration of the iris extends over the yellow-colored part.) There is also a definite difference in their voices — the males have a high whistle and the females a much deeper tone, somewhat of a squawk. The females tend to be larger than the males, but since their plumage is so similar, it can be hard to make quick distinctions based on estimates of relative size. One of the best places to see them up close and to photograph them is near the summit of the trail.

Once you achieve the rim of the crater you are in for a very spectacular view in both directions — down into the crater and out to sea. The crater itself has two layers: a small flat circle not far below where the trail ends, and another layer down much lower. The second level is much larger than the upper one, and your binoculars will help you get a detailed view of the nesting activity going on there.

The "blue-foots" nest on the bright white floors of the crater. When I was there the nesting was not extensive, but there were still dozens of nests, which look like scrapes on the ground with bits of debris placed around their periphery. The occupied nests had quite large young, some showing only bright white fluffy down and others already having in places the dark brown of adult wing feathers. (The nests on the outer edge of the cone seemed less far along; most of the young were very recently hatched, with virtually no feathers showing, or just having a very minimal down development, with no "real" feathers in sight.)

There was an ominous aspect to the scene below, however, as we saw a number of frigate birds patrolling over the crater watching for any young that might be vulnerable to their depredation. It seemed that these young in the crater were too large by now to be easily taken; though they were sitting alone, they were not attacked. (The smaller ones near us seemed to be guarded by an adult at all times.) The frigate birds would cruise, hover a moment over a nest, and then cruise on, casting giant shadows on the birds below them. Then they would ascend, often to the edge of the rim, circle it for awhile, and then go below again, or out to sea.

At one point, I was standing on the rim, changing film and looking down at what I was doing. Suddenly I felt an impact of air, almost like a suction, a vacuum, behind me. I looked up, and rocketing overhead, very close, was one of the frigates. I had felt the wall of air it must have been pushing ahead of it. And I could see every feather distinctly, some raised, some lowered, like a huge collection of flaps stuck to an airplane's wing. And even though it was soaring, not flapping its wings, the flight was the most active thing imaginable. It was working the wind, clawing its way through it — there was nothing "passive" or "fliding" about it.

Young red-footed booby ▶

Another bird that you may well see from the crater rim, either flying around the perimeter of the cone on the ocean side, or spiraling upward from the inner walls of the crater, is the red-billed tropic bird (*Phaetheon aethereus*). They aren't often seen at sea, so a place like this where they nest in crevices in the rock provides one of the few dependable opportunities to see them. One may be sitting on a branch of the scrubby growth inside the crater, or you may see a tail sticking out of a hole among a pile of rocks which conceal its nesting place. And their straight, rapid flight, tail streaming, is a treat to see. It is possible to photograph them in flight, if you're patient enough and quick enough with your camera. You'll probably want to use your telephoto lens for these flight shots. They'll be close, but not right on top of you. Afternoons seem to be a particularly good time to find a number of these birds in the area.

Much less obvious, but very important to the bird-watcher, are the finches of Daphne. A team of ornithologists has been studying them for about a decade. This is one of the few places where birds have been banded, so it is possible to trace the life histories of individual birds over the years. Invaluable knowledge about their breeding habits, feeding patterns and the effects of rain or drought upon their survival rates has all been collected. Sometimes there are some scientists there, and it's a good chance to get a little more information about the birds — and to find out what it's like to live for months on one small and very dry volcanic cone in the middle of the Pacific Ocean.

SEYMOUR NORTE

Seymour Norte is a very busy island. Its location just north of Baltra puts it in the path of every boat. The large boats and even day-trippers from Puerto Ayora are allowed to visit here. (In fact, Baltra is the current name for South Seymour, as Seymour Norte's sister island used to be known.) But it's also a busy nesting place of blue-footed boobies and the Galapagos' largest nesting colony of magnificent frigate birds (*Fregata magnificens*). There are sea lions, swallow-tailed gulls, and maybe you'll even spot a Galapagos snake, as we did on one trip. And though it is not very dramatic, there is a distinct geological difference between this island and many of the others in the archipelago.

The island was formed by uplift of its rocky base from below sea level, rather than by the accumulation of lava and other debris that has formed the characteristically cone-shaped islands that make up most of the islands of the Galapagos. This kind of uplifting of the earth's crust, sometimes bringing the sea bottom high enough that it becomes dry land, is not uncommon in the Islands, though it is by no means the dominant means of land-building, even though all of the islands are made up of volcanic materials. But here the uplift of some ancient, fairly flat flow (formerly under water) has resulted in terrain that is fairly flat, often with a gentle slope in one particular direction. Here on Seymour Norte, the slope falls gradually away from the southern side with the low cliffs which greet the visitor at the landing site.

The landing is sometimes rather difficult, depending on the size of the ocean swell. It's a short leap, aided by a crew member, onto a collection of black boulders that you can scramble up a few meters to reach level ground. The one frustration at the landing point may be that, right there, you might see some swallow-tailed gulls. (They like rock-strewn cliffs, and these low ones seem to have a certain appeal.) Then you may be caught trying to watch your footing, not hold up anyone behind you, and trying to take some pictures very quickly. (You'll probably get a more leisurely look at them on Plaza Sur.)

At first glance, this is one of the most nondescript islands to be visited. However, the variety of Palo Santo that is found on Seymour Norte and Daphne (*Bursera malacophylla*) is endemic to those two islands. It is hairier and more stunted in appearance than its taller relatives on the other islands. Otherwise, you'll see flat ground, gray saltbush of uniform height, and some slightly more open areas with white-splashed rocks. At the beach area there may be young sea lions resting in what shade they can find.

And then, nearly at your feet, you may see your first blue-footed booby at its nest, cocking its golden eye at you, with perhaps a couple of eggs showing beneath it. Or maybe an ugly, gray, naked bag of avian entrails under a shading wing. (It's the whole chick, but in their earliest days they seem to be made mostly of bulbous gut and knife-edge beak.)

SEYMOUR NORTE ISLAND

1. Landing site
2. Palo Santo forest
3. Blue-footed boobies
4. Frigatebird colonies
5. Sea lions, marine iguanas

Blue-footed booby and very young chick

And if there is nesting going on, you will almost certainly be treated to some of the utterly fantastic displays of the birds. The blue feet play a major role in female and male choosing each other, setting up their nest, leaving that nest to feed or loaf, and returning to it without setting off antagonisms or fear. They dip and bow, spread their wings and turn and twist them, paddle the feet to show them off to best advantage. Lots of whistling and squawking goes on as well.

It's not only the adults that do this, either. I have seen young still clothed in down, with only their wings fully feathered, engage in the same types of bowing and wing-spreading and tail-tipping. Is it practice for the future, or just a lot of avian fun?

It will be hard to move on from there, but even though the birds are nearly oblivious to you, standing within arm's reach for long periods of time doesn't seem wise. And there's a lot more to follow, for in a few minutes' more walk you come to the nesting grounds of the magnificent frigate bird.

There are a few of the greater frigate birds that nest there as well. This large and aggressive bird is a "klepto parasite," living off of the work of other birds, stealing their catch from them after vigorous chases in the sky. They have a wingspan of over two meters and they are consummate flyers. In fact, it is hard to believe that a bird that big can be so quick on its

Frigate birds robbing each other of food

wings, so to speak. You may have watched from your boat as it harrasses a gull or booby until the victim drops its catch. Then, before the morsel hits the water, the frigate bird snatches it out of the air and swallows it. (This can happen even if the frigate was *above* the gull at the time of the drop.) Furthermore, if the food sinks more than a few inches into the water, the frigates I saw just left it alone. Diving birds they are not.

You may have seen either the great or magnificent frigate birds engaging in this behavior, but the ones you see at the nests on Seymour Norte are the latter. The females have white going all the way up their front to their chins. The field guide to the birds of the Islands says that the males have a purple sheen to their plumage, particularly on the head (as opposed to a green sheen on the male greater frigate birds). However, it can be pretty hard to distinguish between them in the field. But don't worry about the identification here, because the birds themselves can tell very well, and so can your guide.

These huge birds build their scruffy nests on the tops of the bushes at the farthest extent of the trail (which in its total length, a loop-shape, is only slightly over a kilometer long). If a male does not have a mate yet, he will sit on a nest and watch the females wheeling over. As one comes close overhead he may throw out his wings to their fullest extent, throw back his

head, puff out his garish red throat pouch and shake himself in a frenzy of invitation. However, once a pair has established themselves, whichever one of them is at the nest sits there quietly for the most part, particularly if they already have an egg or chick to care for.

The incongruities are great in this place — the huge dark birds, with their rapacious feeding habits and spectacular flying skills, sitting quietly on low bushes, brooding or feeding young that, except for their long hook-tipped bills, look like they will never grow up to be what their parents are. They are a brilliant fluffy-down white until they are nearly the size of the parents. It will take months of careful nurturing for them to look and act like the patient adult birds that care for them so totally.

To photograph the frigate birds, it is a good idea to bring a moderate telephoto lens as well as a standard one. The birds are big and not far away, but the nesting grounds are extensive and not all sites are occupied at any one time. Therefore, the bird that interests you photographically can be 10 or 15 meters away.

On the trail between the boobies' nesting area and that of the frigate birds there is a place that has a certain local charm. A rock about a meter wide, and a little lower, has a depression in the middle on one side and thus forms a sort of rustic armchair. It is also coated with bird guano, though this is entirely dry and smooth. Local legend has it that when Darwin came to Seymour Norte he sat here, and thus it is known to some as "Darwin's Chair." The problem with this story is that Darwin did not visit Seymour Norte. However, it remains a good place to sit for a moment, think of the great man, and have your picture taken by the guide.

On your way out, if you have been going counter-clockwise on the trail, you will be near the cliffs again. Along the beach itself there may be sea lions, and in the bushes near the shore we once saw a Galapagos snake. It was about 2.5 centimeters in diameter and about a meter long. It, like all snakes on the Islands, is harmless. 🐛

◄ Immature frigate bird

Santiago and Nearby Sites

3

S antiago's numerous visitor sites and its location in the center of the Islands make it one of the most familiar islands of a Galapagos tour. You go from site to site on Santiago, learning about the human history of the Islands as well as seeing the fur seals or Galapagos hawks or boobies diving in Buccaneer Cove. You will take a quick jaunt to Bartolome's Pinnacle Rock, or pull into the quiet cove of Sombrero Chino to anchor in a storm. But wherever you go around the island, the cone of Santiago's Sugarloaf or the sweep of black volcanic rock on its shores will appear again and again, giving you a visual anchor for a major part of your visit.

Santiago also may be the jumping-off point for the very long trip northeast to Genovesa, home of the red-footed boobies and thousands of storm petrels.

Santiago (San Salvador, James)

S antiago (James) is an island that your itinerary is likely to bring you back to several times. Its visitor sites are on the east and west sides of the island, and its relatively central location in the whole Galapagos archipelago means that your route will often pass it as you criss-cross to the more distant islands or to the numerous visitor sites on nearby islands.

This island has powerful evocations of past human use, including the extraordinary ravages of introduced goats and the remains of several attempts at salt mining. It also has some of the most impressive natural sites — the fur seal grottos, a flamingo lagoon, and the very recent lava flows at Sullivan Bay. At each of the sites, bird-watching is particularly rewarding, with sightings of flamingos, Galapagos hawks or vermilion flycatchers likely.

JAMES BAY

This bay, on the northeast side of Santiago, is a lovely stopping place in itself; but its chief function is the starting point for four visitor sites: Sugarloaf, the salt crater, the fur seal grottos, and Espumilla Beach with its flamingo lagoon. The first three are reached from the same anchorage, and Espumilla Beach is a short boat ride to the northern end of the bay.

◄ Top: Motor sailer in James Bay. Bottom: View at the beginning of the path on Bartolome Island. *Tiguilia* plants on the slope

Before moving to the visitor sites themselves, it's worth noting that this bay usually offers a particularly good chance to savor the sea life around you. If you are there in the early morning or later afternoon, go sit out on deck and watch what goes on around the boat. The boobies plunge for fish, the pelicans dive and then swim along the surface, followed closely by the brown noddies who hope for fish spilling out of the pelicans' pouches. Sometimes a noddy even sits on a pelican's head, in order to be really close to the action. Sally Lightfoot crabs scuttle over the exposed black rocks near the shoreline. (They're especially easy to see on the one rock

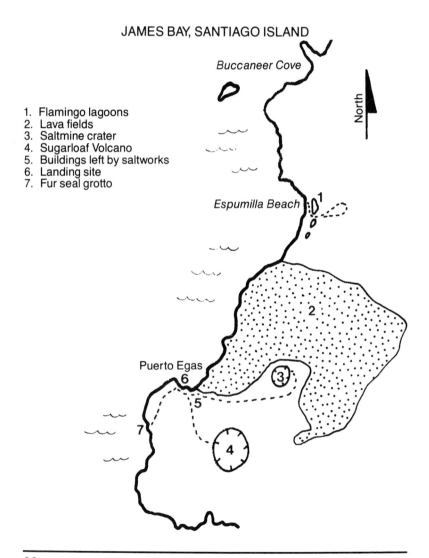

JAMES BAY, SANTIAGO ISLAND

Buccaneer Cove

North

1. Flamingo lagoons
2. Lava fields
3. Saltmine crater
4. Sugarloaf Volcano
5. Buildings left by saltworks
6. Landing site
7. Fur seal grotto

Espumilla Beach

Puerto Egas

protruding, fingerlike, above the surface near the point where you will disembark.)

When I was there in an El Nino year, this anchorage was the place where I saw the most storm petrels (*Oceanodroma castro*) at once, flitting and dipping over the water's surface as they fed. The water was so calm that in the flat light of evening it gleamed as though dark oil had been poured on it. Only these tiny birds, themselves nearly completely black, relieved the unbroken somberness as I peered down onto the water.

SUGARLOAF — HIKE UP THE MOUNTAIN
(description by Elizabeth Greene)

Sugarloaf is the taller of the pair of volcanic cones that dominate the horizon of James Bay. It rises 450 meters above sea level. The trip up is a short, but fairly grueling hike and few visitors attempt it. (It is a good test for the hike up Alcedo—see Isla Isabela. If this hike is too hard, you won't want to try Alcedo.)

Usually the guide has a good sense of whether any of the group would be interested in or capable of doing the hike, but don't hesitate to consult your guide if you're ambitious—and hardy. The schedule may allow a try.

The gradual approach to the base of Sugarloaf is about one kilometer long. It is very likely that some of the goats that damage Santiago so greatly will be evident along the way. On the more positive side, the trail passes an intermittent rivulet of fresh water that runs down the side of the cone. The water is a gathering place for the Galapagos dove, the finches and many other birds.

Once past this place, the going gets a bit rough. The ascent becomes quite steep and the ground underfoot is shale-like and slippery. Near the top it may be necessary to locomote on all fours. But the terrain does level off somewhat at the very last and the view from the very top is thoroughly rewarding.

The crater itself is about 200 meters deep, and sometimes has a little water in it. If your next destination is the salt crater, the route proceeds about one-quarter of the way around the crater rim. (It is very slippery and dusty on the higher levels and hikers tend to shuffle and slide down quite quickly.) Otherwise you return the way you came. The hike can take from two to four hours, round trip.

PUERTO EGAS — THE SALT CRATER

After a wet landing the visitor walks a few dozen meters to the area used until the 1950s as a port for a salt extraction operation started decades ago by a Señor Egas. From this area the view is rather bleak: a collection of rusted hulks of old machinery and the remains of posts from defunct sheds.

The trail, which actually follows the remnants of a road wagons once

Overlooking the salt crater

used to haul the salt, starts to wind away from the shore and up around the slopes of the crater's cone. It's hard to get much of a sense of the topography at first; there's just a slope on your left side and flat ground to the immediate right. It's an easy walk, though on a very hot day it can seem a lot longer than it is. Wear tennis shoes, not sandals; light-weight slacks are also a good idea. Somehow this hike seems to be one of the hottest excursions. The way to minimize discomfort is to keep a close eye on the sights alongside you as you walk, and don't be impatient just to reach the rim of the salt crater itself.

Depressing though it may be, it is likely that the ravages of goats upon the land will be very clear here. The bushes, many two meters high, look like they've had an extremely amateurish haircut, in the bowl-over-the-head style. That is, there will be no leaves up to your own head height, and then there will be a cap of intact green leaves. The goats can easily feed by standing on their hind legs, and that green cap marks the limit of the goats' chewing reach!

If you happen to see the goats themselves, you will notice that they are extremely wary. They act like the wild animals we are used to in most other places — whether in parks or unprotected areas. They will look at you, a bit curious for a moment, and then seem to melt away from view. It is easy to see why eradicating them is such a difficult task, with these smart, tough animals living in this pitted, rugged terrain which offers unlimited opportunities for escape and hiding.

But move along; as the elevation gradually increases, the bird-watchers in the group are probably in for some great moments. The slope of the crater is a likely place to see the vermilion flycatcher (*Pyrocephalus rubinus*). Just as it stands out in the dark greenery of the Highlands of Santa Cruz, this bird makes a stark and beautiful contrast here with the grey Palo Santo trees that clothe the slopes of Santiago. It will be sitting on a branch, head and chest red beyond imagining, and then it will launch itself out into the air to snap at an insect too small and too fast for a human eye to see. The click of its bill as it makes the catch is how you'll know he's succeeded (or she, if it is the more subtly colored buff-and-brown female). Then the bird circles back to its original perch, having completed a circle perhaps a meter in diameter.

With luck, the large-billed flycatcher (*Myarchus magnirostris*) will be seen there, too. Its colors are not as spectacular, but its similar feeding habits are just as interesting.

And the trail is usually rich with finches, too. I saw the warbler finch here once, and the unique woodpecker finch, the dream of anyone interested in bird behavior. Once I saw one pecking into a tree. I went closer, thinking, "Could *this* be the woodpecker finch?" As I got closer, I saw that it had a spine in its bill, a cactus-like spine, about an inch long! And it was using the spine to probe into the tree! I was just completely amazed by this —to actually see something that I'd read about and seen on TV... how an animal uses a tool!

Then it dropped that spine and came back with quite a wobbly-looking one, crooked, with little wisps coming off it (not a spine, in other words). After the bird tried probing with it a couple of times, to no avail because it would bend, it dropped that twig and went off to another tree that had thorns and picked one of those. That one seemed to work.

There is another birding event that can happen on this trail: an appearance of the Galapagos hawk, at the end of the trail, just as you come out onto open ground at the rim of the crater. It can be quite windy there, and the hawks seem to like this place for tossing themselves around in the wind currents overhead—that is, when they're not sitting quietly on one of the nearby tree branches staring down at the visitors.

There, at the rim of the salt crater, are marvelous sights on both sides. First, there is the crater itself. Its volcano is long extinct, and its floor is about 10 meters below sea level. Evidently salt water seeps in slowly through cracks in the rock; as it comes up in the crater itself, a shallow, briny lake is formed. The fierce sun evaporates the surface water and the remains can be collected as usable salt. Several efforts have been made to create a viable business of this, but none have succeeded.

It's possible at times to see remains of impoundments that were made for drying the salt further, cutting the circular lake into pie-shaped wedges. The edges are usually a brilliant white, and the center may be white or tan or a bright green, depending on the water level and the growth of algae. Look closely for a flamingo or two in the distance; you may be lucky.

You will be seeing here a scene that Darwin described in his *Voyage of the Beagle*. He reports:

> One day we accompanied a party of the Spaniards in their whale-boat to a salina, or lake from which salt is procured. After landing, we had a very rough walk over a rugged field of recent lava, [Obviously he took a different route than the modern visitor takes.] which has almost surrounded a tuff-crater, at the bottom of which the salt-lake lies.
>
> The water is only three or four inches deep, and rests on a layer of beautifully crystallized, white salt. The lake is quite circular, and is fringed with a border of bright green succulent plants; the almost precipitous walls of the crater are clothed in wood, so that the scene was altogether both picturesque and curious. A few years since, the sailors belonging to a sealing-vessel murdered their captain in this quiet spot; and we saw his skull lying among the bushes.

Today's visitor isn't allowed to go down into the crater, to see if the skull is still there, or to see the salt crystals up close. You will see clearly from the rim, across the crater, the remains of the road that was constructed more recently to bring out the salt. Now it's just a pale gash, gracefully winding around half of the crater's interior slope.

If you turn in the other direction, looking directly away from the crater's center, you face wave upon wave of black and orange lava fields. These vast sweeps of contrastingly colored earth very much characterize the vistas on the island. The older flows — the orange ones — have a fair amount of vegetation scattered over them. The stark gray of the Palo Santo trees is broadcast over the orange slopes as far as the eye can see. Once again it's easy to understand how the goats find ample cover in this tortured terrain. The black flows seem utterly barren, and only a much closer examination allows the visitor to see that, even here, plant and animal life exist.

THE FUR SEAL GROTTOS

The fur seal grottos are only a 700-meter walk from the same landing used for Puerto Egas. The level, sandy trail is off to the right, roughly following the edge of the island, but a few meters in from the somewhat rocky shore. The trail here is very good for bird-watching. There may be Galapagos hawks; often there are shorebirds feeding on tidbits along the wave-splashed rocks.

Here I saw the oystercatcher (*Haematopus ostralegus*), most impressive with its black and white plumage, red bill, yellow-ringed eye and ugly pink feet. Three whimbrels flew overhead once, and finches are common in the nearby brush. It's worth checking any vegetation growing at shoreline to see if the yellow warbler is feeding there. I saw them most often in these circumstances, their yellow showing up clearly against the green of the damp seaweed.

Young sea lion

The rocks, in places, are also packed with marine iguanas. Your guide will point out the first ones you encounter. They pile on each other in layers, two or even three deep. They seem to compete with each other for the spot that has the most direct exposure to the sun, even if it means clinging nearly vertically from a shoreline boulder, with tails hanging out into space.

The walk will be an easy 15 minutes, ending at a small plain of black lava flow. This area is pocked by three aquamarine "potholes." These holes are formed in the same way that the Santa Cruz lava tubes were formed, only these are not land-locked. The lava flow went out to the open sea and now the water rushes in and out of the tubes with the tides. They are often deep enough for swimming, with their depth varying from perhaps 3 to 10 meters. Before you swim there, however, consult with your guide about the tide flow conditions. Swimming can be extremely easy; snorkeling among the fish and fur seals adds a wonderful dimension. However, if the tides are changing, or the water is high, swimming can be very risky. Swimmers have been dashed against the very jagged walls, or thrown up against the underside of the "bridges," with painful and frightening results.

But if swimming conditions are right, a brief dip there will be one of the highlights of your trip. The main two pools are connected to each other, with a bridge of black lava arching over them near the middle of their length. The exit of the pool to the open sea also has an arch over it, where it's great just to sit and watch the water flow back and forth below you.

Lava rock bridge next to the open ocean by the fur seal grottos

You'll have company here. The fur seals will be lounging around at the edges of the pools. You'll have to be careful not to disturb these rather small and cuddly mammals as you descend into the water by a short set of natural steps. And there may be fur seals right in there with you as you swim. Seals may swish past with total ease and nonchalance, sometimes giving human swimmers a real surprise as they quietly float at the surface and peer at the array of colorful tropical fish that share these grottos.

The grottos are only about 15 meters long, but for sheer beauty and ease of access, there are few places on the island that can compete. Black rocks, crystal clear blue water, fur seals and tropical fish—and each year I was there, I saw what must have been the same yellow-crowned night heron on exactly the same rock, just a step below the rim of the largest pool. It was like some welcoming sign, confirming for the visitor that all was well.

ESPUMILLA BEACH

Espumilla Beach, at the northern shore of James Bay, has historic significance. Just north of it is a source of fresh water, much prized by pirates who plied these waters centuries ago. Now visitors go there for the quiet beach and the lagoons that are located just over the ridge of land and bush behind the beach. This is a likely place for seeing flamingos, if you approach carefully enough. I've seen common stilts there, and white-cheeked pintails.

There is a 2-kilometer trail that goes inland from the lagoon. It makes a slight ascent over a knob of land and then loops back to its starting point. There will be several species of finch to see, perhaps vermilion fly-catchers, and even some of those pestiferous goats.

BUCCANEER COVE

Buccaneer Cove is less than an hour's sail north of James Bay and Espumilla Beach. On my three visits we didn't land there—there's a beach area, but no trails or set destinations. You may anchor overnight or just go into the cove so your guide can tell you about its human history. That's important, but be sure to take a good look at the scenery—it's spectacular.

The cove served generations of pirates and then whalers as a safe harbor near one of the few fresh-water sources in the Islands. They would land, take on water, perhaps kill a few of the goats for fresh meat, and gather firewood for the ship's galley. Remains of ceramic vessels have been found submerged offshore—anti-litter campaigns certainly had no meaning in those days.

Now the cove can give a few vicarious chills at the thought of these men, living at the edges of human law and their own physical endurance. But it also can give a very immediate sense of awe as you look up at the vast, vertical walls, especially on the north side, which encompass much of the cove. The cove is the remnant of a volcano which formed at the edge of the island. You can trace the layers upon layers of volcanic debris that have been deposited over time. Sometimes there were explosions that expelled tons of fine materials, which settled back around the central vent and built up the walls of the crater. Other layers are composed of molten lava that pushed up more slowly and partially filled the crater's depths.

Winds, rain and the invading ocean have eroded the cove walls to leave some of the most dramatic scenery in the islands. On the south wall in particular are the multi-hued strata that tell of the cone's growth and erosion. All along the north wall there are great pockmarks and caves and finger-like vertical protrusions. Here the wall's deep browns and ochres are splashed with the white of bird excrement—an undignified source of quite lovely visual accents. And frigate birds and boobies sit peering out to sea, or launch themselves out for a fishing sortie. Your boat will probably come very close to the wall to give you a good view. The closeness may be a bit nerve-wracking, but your guide will probably explain that the cliffs are as perpendicular below the surface as above and that the water there is very deep indeed. So be sure to be out on deck with binoculars and camera and be ready to take in these brief but spectacular moments.

SULLIVAN BAY — THE LAVA FLOWS

As your boat passes by Santiago on its various trips, and as it pulls into Sullivan Bay itself, you often see wedges of black lava cutting across the island's reddish slopes. Santiago is a classic volcanic island, rising to a dominant cone nearly 1000 meters tall at its northwest "corner." It also has many smaller cones projecting from its major slope, some having craters and others not.

Sullivan Bay is the place where the agedness of the Islands is suddenly brought very much up to date; for here is a lava flow only about 90 years old. It is a great swath of black rock that oozed down to the sea, curling around small cones that came before it, adding land at the sea's edge where there was no land before. There is a lot to be learned here about land-building processes, but first there is the feeling of astonishment and mystery as you walk over the shiny black lava fields.

The landing is a dry one, onto a small ledge. You should wear lightweight running shoes to protect your feet on landing, and on the fairly smooth but sun-baked lava flow. (Your guide may have wear-toughened feet, but visitors rarely do.) Watch for penguins near the landing area.

As you enter the lava field, what looks from a distance to be monotonous paving turns out to be a multi-level terrain of sheer fascination. It is like being in immobile black batter—110 square kilometers of it. The proper name for this kind of flow is pahoehoe, pronounced with five syllables—pa-

New black lava flow on older volcanic slope. Bartolome Pinnacle in the background

Top left:
Masked booby

Bottom left:
White-banded angle-fish,
eating a banana skin

Bottom right:
Female lava lizard in breeding
colors

Top:
Male frigate bird displaying
to female flying overhead

Bottom:
Mustard rays

OPPOSITE:

Top left:
Mullugo flavescens, arid lowlands,
early colonizer of lava flows

Top right:
Pelican viewing James Bay

Center:
Sally Lightfoot crabs

Bottom:
Galapagos dove

OPPOSITE:

Top:
Flamingo and white-cheeked pintail

Bottom left:
Land iguana in rich vegetation of El Nino year

Bottom right:
Cliffs with swallow-tailed gulls

Top:
Boat crew member with langousta — a warm water "lobster"

Bottom:
Greater frigate bird female cooling off

OPPOSITE:

Top:
Blue-footed booby (favorite photo)

Center:
Vermilion flycatcher waiting for
tortoise to stir up insects

Bottom left:
Sea lion and pup in waves at
Rabida Island

Bottom right:
Darwin's finch

Top:
Sesuvium in lava rocks

Bottom:
Rancher on boundary between
agricultural land and park reserve

Top left:
Bottle-nosed dolphin (porpoise)

Bottom left:
Saddle-backed tortoise at Charles Darwin
Research Station

Bottom right:
American oystercatcher near fur seal grottos

SULLIVAN BAY, SANTIAGO ISLAND
& BARTOLOME ISLAND

1. Landing sites
2. Lava flow, circa 1900
3. Old eroded lava flow
4. Pinnacle Rock
5. Beach
6. Summit trail
7. Viewpoint
8. Spatter cones

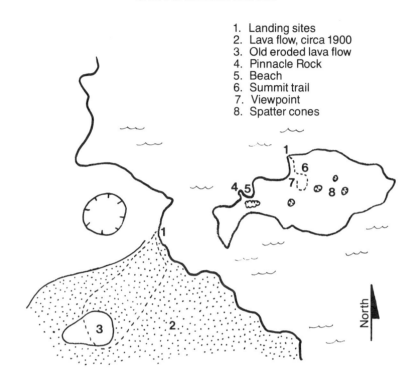

ho-e, ho-e. The word is Hawaiian for "ropy." Used to describe the same type of lava flow and surface character, it is used today by scientists. It is a very apt word, conveying very well the shapes the lava takes as it flows fairly slowly, hardening into fans and swirls and protrusions of roughly parallel, rope-shaped strands.

This kind of pattern is formed when the superheated lava cools more rapidly on its surface than in its interior. The lower, hotter part continues to flow and the upper parts begin to "drag" as they cool and harden. This uneven cooling gives the flowing mass its characteristic fan shape, with a series of curving creases roughly perpendicular to the direction of the flow. The relative flatness of the land over which it flows (the lava tends to separate and flow around obstacles like earlier-established volcanic cones) and the fact that this flow went rather slowly overall—it was not the result of explosive volcano-building —allowed the flow to meander.

So there are fans of a few inches in diameter as well as ones several meters across; they all interweave and overlap in the most marvelous fashion. Some of them look very much like other things—one part you're likely to see is the one called "pig guts" by the locals, and there's no arguing the accuracy. (Other names are more elegant, some less.)

There are various levels of this huge gleaming surface, evidently because of the build-up of gases below, which could raise a section and then let it drop as the gas cooled. There are some very large cracks, where you can see down to other layers of rock—the average depth of the whole field is two meters. Some cracks take a bit of a jump to get across; or you can just follow the crack to its end and keep going in a slightly different direction.

Another intriguing part of this flow is the plant life, past and present. Where the flowing lava encountered a plant, especially a woody section of

Lava bubbles in the pahoehoe flow

Lava cactus *(Brachycereus nesioticus)*

one, it flowed around and quickly vaporized the encased plant. However, in a few cases, the plant lasted long enough to leave a clear imprint, sometimes completely in the round (or hollow) of its shape. There is something rather eerie about this quick immortalizing process.

The lava flow is also a lesson in plant colonization. The flow is so recent, the rock so hard, and the rainfall so scarce that there is virtually no organic material, much less true soil. Yet there are plants scattered here and there on the stark surface. The most obvious plant is a form of cactus called the lava cactus *(Brachycereus nesioticus)*. It looks like a fistful of very prickly cucumbers joined together at the base and then fanning outward and upward for 10 to 25 centimeters or so. The growing tips tend to be a bright straw color, with the older base being dark gray.

The other early colonizer of the nearly soil-less lava flow is the "carpetweed" plant *(Mollugo flavescens)*. It forms a network of wispy stems that hug the surface of the lava and spread out only 15 or 20 centimeters. Sometimes its tiny flowers are visible.

If there is little plant life to be seen here, there is even less animal life. There may be the painted locust, a very colorful grasshopper *(Schistocerca melanocera)*, and you may see some goat droppings; but for the most part, flies and lava lizards are just about it — the latter preying upon the former.

As you walk inland, it is possible to see what this flow may look like many thousands of years from now. At the edges of the black tongues of new lava there actually is soil — though it is very coarse soil. This soil has oxidized to a rich rust color. Plants have taken hold and there is sparse

shrubbery, none of it very high. Take a walk out onto the older ground and look back at the lava. Think what it was like 90 or so years ago, to hear and smell and see that lava oozing toward you. Was it fast, or would it have been easy to step out of its path, and head for the safety of that low hillock? No one was there at the time, but someone might be there next time. 🐛

Tower (Genovesa)

Tower is a small island (10.5 square kilometers) at the upper righthand "corner" of the Galapagos archipelago. It is not visited as often as the more central islands because of the length of the voyage and the relative roughness of the long trip in open seas. There are two visitor sites on the island: the beach and tidepool area around Darwin Bay, and the inland area reached from the bay by what are known as "Prince Philip's Steps." Both sites are particularly good for seeing interesting birdlife.

Darwin Bay

After an easy wet landing there is a short walk up the brilliant white coral beach to a rather bizarre area of inland tide pools and rugged outcroppings of black rock, over head-height. The greenery edging the pools is the salt bush (*Cryptocarpus pyriformis*), or "monte salado," as it is known in Spanish. These pools are feeding sites for shorebirds such as wandering tattlers, turnstones, whimbrels and lava gulls (which nest in the cliffs of the island, as do swallow-tailed gulls). Yellow-crowned, lava and black-crowned night herons are found there, too, though the last-named are fairly rare.

And, while warblers are certainly not considered to be shorebirds, it is common to see the yellow warbler probing along the edges of the tidepool for the little fiddler crabs and other minute shore life. (In fact, the majority of times when I saw the yellow warbler in the Galapagos, it has been right at the shoreline, pecking and probing among the vegetation there.)

Here or at other places on the island you may see lava gulls, which nest on the cliffs and the west side of the bay, and swallow-tailed gulls, which nest on the cliffs of the eastern side.

The trail follows the line of the bay until it reaches higher and more arid ground, but you may find yourself completely occupied by the bird life you see at first. When I was there we saw dozens of great frigate birds (*Fregata minor*) on nests, and loafing on the rocks and shrubs. It was during a year of the heavy rain and severe heat of the El Nino current. The temperature on land that morning must have been at least 30 degrees C. We humans could hardly keep walking — there was no breeze behind the huge boulders that lined that part of the bay.

The birds were suffering as well. Many of them were sitting in the most grotesque positions, apparently trying to maximize their cooling.

◀ Returning down Prince Philip's Steps to the boat

Some sat hunched on a branch, heads dropping very far down on chests, wings turned with the underside out. Others sat on the nearly vertical sides of rocks, with heads up and tails spread out almost like shovels, and their wings were bent so that they looked like they had their "arms akimbo," also exposing the inner lining of the wings.

Some of the birds were on nests, though there were no young in sight. Rather, the males seemed to be trying very hard simply to attract a mate. This was where we got the best view of the display of their outspread wings, inflated pouch and whinnying whistles as they tried to communicate with females flying overhead. With these huge birds and their contorted postures, the glaring of white sand and black rock, the heat that seemed to be baking our brains, this visit had a rather nightmarish quality, as though we were on the edge of delirium. Even the water at that time was too warm to offer real relief. You probably won't run into that kind of heat, but then the birds may not be doing such strange things, either. No two visits are alike — virtually all are fascinating.

PRINCE PHILIP'S STEPS

The landing for this site is a dry one. The so-called "steps" are actually a rather steep, 25-meter scramble up a cleft in the cliffs on the east side of Darwin Bay. They were given their name after a visit by Britain's Prince Philip in 1964.

Once you reach level ground, there is a wealth of varied bird life. One of the first species you may see is the red-footed booby, which nests on the low bushes here. After seeing all those blue-footed and masked boobies nesting on the ground, it seems quite incongruous to see their tree-borne counterparts perched above you, their luminous red webbed feet curled over the branches they sit on. About 95 percent of the red-foots are a dark beige; the other 5 percent are quite white. Both plumage types are the same species.

Scattered over the island are nests of the masked booby, as well, which make use of several kinds of terrain for nesting. In general, their breeding season lasts from September to July. They, too, have elaborate and almost bizarre territorial, mate-selection, and nest-maintenance displays, rivaling that of their blue- and red-footed relatives.

The scrubby flatlands are also the home of four species of finch. The large ground finch of Tower is distinctive for having the heaviest bill of any of its species (the same species showing marked differences in some cases, depending on which island or islands it primarily resides). The other finches are the sharp-beaked ground finch, the large cactus finch and the warbler finch.

In amongst these birds can be found the Galapagos dove and the Tower race of the Galapagos mockingbird — the smallest race of this particular species. There may be nesting great frigate birds established in the tops of the shrubs and small trees, as well, depending on the season. A few of the magnificent frigates nest on the island, too.

After you pass through the scrub brush, the trail comes out to the edge of a large lava field that stretches out before you to the sea. At first it will look like there is nothing to see; but then you will notice a small creature fluttering low over the lava, and then another. Suddenly you realize that you're seeing the constant movement of hundreds and even thousands of tiny storm petrels circling and twisting in flight. You may see thousands more offshore, like clouds of avian mosquitoes.

Both the wedge-rumped storm petrel (Galapagos storm petrel, *Oceanodroma tethys*) and the band-rumped storm petrel (Madeiran storm petrel, *Oceanodroma castro*) nest in crannies and tunnels beneath the rugged lava field surface.

> *Nothing could look more dreary, yet there is a teeming city beneath the arid surface.... There is here a huge colony of petrels.... Beneath the lava crust they must inhabit a maze of cavities and tunnels, for one hears a constant muted churring and calling and occasionally a petrel squeezes out of a crack and flies off. Overhead they flit about like a cloud of midges, twisting, turning, fluttering and sweeping out to the cliff edge and back again. (Nelson, pp. 96–97)*

From the low crest of ground where you stand to see the lava field there are deep and narrow cracks in the earth that harbor one of the major

DARWIN BAY, TOWER ISLAND

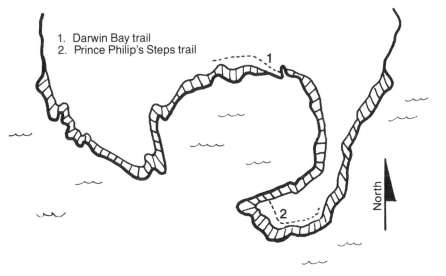

1. Darwin Bay trail
2. Prince Philip's Steps trail

North

predators of the petrel, particularly the young ones — the short-eared owl (*Asio flammeus*). It hunts both day and night, but when I saw one it was just sitting quietly at the lip of one of the cracks, just a few meters away. Others have observed and written about them over the years.

> *Scattered over the lava in shady recesses there are many sinister owls'*
> *"parlours" containing the skulls, bones and feathers of scores of petrels,*
> *which probably form the main diet of several pairs of owls preying*
> *constantly on the colony. (Nelson, p. 97)*

Finally, from your crest vantage point, the view of bird life flying along the cliffs can be very rewarding. Red-billed tropic birds, blue-footed boobies in platoons, Audubon's shearwaters (*Puffinus lherminieri*) and noddy terns (*Anous stolidus*) may all be seen, complemented by frigates and perhaps red-footed and masked boobies returning from far-away fishing sorties.

Bartolome (Bartholomew)

T his is the single most-visited place in the Galapagos. If you saw just one photograph of the Islands before you came, it probably was of Bartolome's Pinnacle Rock, towering over a perfect blue cove, lined by a copper-colored beach, and set off by the rugged profile of Santiago not far in the distance.

Red-billed tropic bird on nest in rocky crevice

The Pinnacle rock on Bartolome

There are two sites on this small island—a hike up an extinct lava cone for a sweeping view of the nearby islands, and a beach where snorkeling and bird watching can be very good.

SUMMIT TRAIL

The landing for the summit trail is a dry one, directly from the panga onto a rock-and-concrete stairway from water level. The trail is 600 meters one way, and it is a continuous and fairly steep ascent. Almost anyone can do it, if care is taken. You do not need hiking boots, just comfortable running shoes and socks. The trail is very wide; in fact, it is used so much that the gritty lava tuff is being eroded at a rapid rate. The trail gets deeper and wider by the month. This heavy erosion is exacerbated by the influx of day-trippers from Puerto Ayora. Boats which carry 30 to 50 people at a time come here just for the day and the site evidently cannot support the extensive use. The main season for this kind of travel is mid-July to the end of August (While it will not help slow down the erosion, planning your visit to avoid these months can result in a less crowded experience in heavily visited central core island sites. It will be interesting to see what response the Park makes to this problem.)

You slog through what feels like heavy sand, and then the last 100 meters have a rough log staircase to help the visitor and to try to retard destruction of the slope. That stairway comes just in time, but it was apparently made for a race of giants; lots of people go around each log, thus increasing the wear and tear on the slope. It's one of the most obvious cases of the problems that arise when one fragile area has great importance both for conservation and visitor use.

At the same time, you will be struck by the stark beauty around you. The gracefulness of the contours contrasts with the near-barrenness of the slope on which you climb. As you look closer, you will see the little lava lizards scampering across the ground, or sitting on one of the small boulders that were blasted out of the throat of the now-extinct volcano that formed the island.

Scattered at distant but regular intervals will be wispy plants, spreading themselves out to maximize access to moisture. They serve an important function in these conditions by stabilizing the ground in which they put down their roots. The two spreading ones are *Chamaesyce amplexicaulis*, which has greenish stems, and *Tiquilia nesiotica*, the more thinly spreading of the two, which has grayish stems. And you will see that early colonizer of sere surfaces, the lava cactus (*Brachycereus nesioticus*).

As you follow the path, you soon come to a number of "spatter cones" on both sides of the trail. These are very large intrusions of lava through the gravelly tuff slopes. Some of the cones are rather flat at the top, with mini-craters within. Some rise up 5 or 10 meters and seem to have had one side stripped away. They are strikingly colored, with deep reds and iridescent blacks and deep greens blending into each other.

Nearer the top you can see that the island has dozens of these cones, in various stages of erosion. There are lava tubes, too, in differing sizes and in various states of preservation. They look like twisting tram lines from far above. Overall, the island can make you feel like you are on the surface of the moon, with craters scattered in every direction. The water is so clear that you can see more of them near the shore, and you realize that the bay is, in fact, simply an underwater crater, somewhat larger than many of those dotting the land.

The wind will probably be picking up as you reach the very top of the island, so you'll be glad if you brought a windbreaker here. There are several flat areas on which to stand and look all around you. There is nowhere else on the islands where you can get such a strong sense of the sheer numbers and variety of sizes of the islands of the Galapagos. The nearest island you can see is Santiago, a few minutes away by boat. South are Santa Cruz, Baltra and Seymour Norte. Rabida is to the southwest. And there are dozens of islets and large rocks protruding from the ocean's surface.

The larger islands are dramatically colored, with the typical orange base, the sweeps of black lava, the fringes of gray plant life. The ocean's color ranges from nearly white at shorelines to turquoise to blue and gun-metal gray. The profiles of the land, the contours and dimensions are endlessly fascinating and quite beautiful. Pinnacle Rock (about 70 meters

Overview of both beaches on Bartolome

Descending the summit trail

high) at the mouth of the cove sets off the scene admirably. The top of the island is very far above it, on a level with the frigate birds that use it as a roost between their raids on other birds.

Naturally you'll want your camera. Polarizing filters are a must here, so that you at least can choose whether you want the underwater craters to show or not. There is likely to be very strong glare, whether the day is clear or overcast. For portraying the scenery here, both a wide-angle and a normal lens will be necessary. For the wildlife, it's mostly lava lizards, so a 100- to 200-mm lens should do fine.

THE BEACHES

When you make the easy, but wet, landing at the beach at Bartolome, you will be on the north side of a narrow neck of land that stretches between the larger section of the island—where you probably just climbed to the top — and the smaller section, from which Pinnacle Rock soars. From the shore there is a 100-meter walk to the beach on the far side. Of interest on the walk are the plants that take hold on the upper reaches of many Galapagos beaches: red and white mangrove, salt bush, morning glory and prickly pear. The path is not wide, but it is clear and you won't have to dodge too many spines or brushy slaps in the face.

Ghost crab

Once on the south side you may see sea turtles, if it is in their nesting season. This is one of the beaches where they lay their eggs (January to March). Your guide will help you spot where they have laid eggs under the sand, and you will be able to go around them. Those turtles don't need any more problems with survival than they have already!

There may be great blue herons stalking along the shoreline. It is also worthwhile to give a careful squint down into the water, for it is not uncommon to see sharks cruising the shallows.

Back at the north beach, you will probably have a chance to go swimming. The cove is an excellent spot for snorkeling; the submerged rocks and underwater ridges have a wide variety of undersea life. And you are still quite near shore and in fairly shallow water. And don't forget to look on the rocky shore near the Pinnacle for some penguins. There may be two or three and they are wonderful to see.

Other Islands: Sombrero Chino, Rabida

SOMBRERO CHINO

A visit to this small island is likely to be an easy-going, comfortable and surprisingly interesting time. Sombrero Chino ("the Chinese hat") is just 200 meters away from the southeast coast of Santiago, not far from the Bainbridge Rocks. The island is nestled into a protective curve of Santiago's shore and this creates a quiet channel for boats to anchor in. Your boat may stay there more than once, because of the island's location on the crossroads between the much-visited islands of Santa Cruz and Santiago, and because it is a refuge if the sea is stormy.

For the actual landing on Sombrero Chino itself, the panga will take you to a lovely crescent-shaped beach with bright white sand. It's a wet landing, though not difficult. Right away you may be amongst sea lions, lolling as they do on the beach or on the sandy patches scattered along the rocky shore.

The trail is only about 350 meters long. It ends at a very rocky point where waves crash in a most spectacular fashion. The path is close to the shore and is an easy walk, though sturdy shoes are a good idea because of the intermittent rockiness.

The volcanic origin of the island is very clear. There are the remains of several types of lava flow here, and numerous small lava tubes, some only centimeters in diameter. Many are broken and rather rough to walk on. There are patches of pahoehoe lava, the relatively smooth ropy lava. It is very black and shiny. In tiny pockets that have accumulated a bit of soil, you will see one of the early colonizers of lava flows, the plant *Sesuvium edmunstonei*. Its leaves are thick and fleshy and look more like branching stems than the leaves on shrubs in moister environments. In the driest time of the year the leaves are a rose color that almost glows against the black rock. The stems hug the rock as they branch out 40 to 50 centimeters.

RABIDA ISLAND

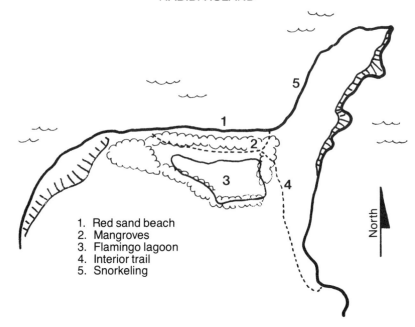

1. Red sand beach
2. Mangroves
3. Flamingo lagoon
4. Interior trail
5. Snorkeling

North

The shoreline has a number of rocky protrusions that are much loved by pelicans. You should have some great chances to photograph them. The shore itself is very rich. It teems with Sally Lightfoot crabs. How their brilliant oranges and blues stand out against the wet, black rocks!

And on the inland side is the Sombrero itself, rising above you with its rust-red sides, punctuated by the light grays of the Palo Santo and of the more shrub-like spreading *Tiquilia nesiotica*. The low light of early morning or late evening seems to bring out the best of the contrasting colors of rock and plant on the slopes of the now-silent volcano.

RABIDA

At first glance, Rabida is another typical beach-plus-mangrove-plus-flamingo lagoon site. But what makes it very different and very memorable is the color of the beach and island soil: a rich russet that gleams in the sun and gives everything on it a special quality of soft beauty.

The island is an hour and a half by boat from Sombrero Chino. It is small, just a little over 2 kilometers across at its widest point. It is steep and rugged and rises to over 400 meters at its highest point, though the visitor will be staying at the lowest elevations. The chief vegetation on the slopes is opuntia cactus, Palo Santo trees and other scrubby bushes. Right at the shoreline there is the band of mangrove that separates the beach itself from the salt water lagoon inland just a few meters.

The landing is a wet one, onto the narrow strip of beach. There usually are a number of sea lions there on the beach or in the small caves that have been formed in the cliffs at the water's edges. Even if you see no sea lions basking or swimming at the beach, your nose will tell you if they are still to be found a little farther on. Be careful when you walk into the mangrove strip because the sea lions also love to sleep in the shade of the bushes. It is entirely possible to unexpectedly step on an extended flipper. An irritated sea lion can move amazingly quickly and inflict quite a bite, so caution is called for.

It takes only a minute or two to reach the lagoon. With any luck at all there will be flamingos sieving through the brackish water for the minute plant and animal life that they depend on for food. Each time I was there we also saw several of the Galapagos white-cheeked pintail ducks (*Anas bahamensis*). This is a very attractive bird with a steel-blue bill decorated by fuchsia stripes along its lower length.

At the far end of the lagoon (to your right, facing inland) is another strip of mangroves, nestling against the hillside. This is a nesting area for pelicans. One August, I saw several of them with their fluffy white offspring. Masked and blue-footed boobies nest on cliffs in this area as well.

If you have time, your group may continue past the lagoon and up a slight slope to a cliff that overlooks a small ocean inlet. The walk will take only 15 or 20 minutes. It is a very easy walk (bring your running shoes for this), though there is no shade; on really hot days, the walk can be a bit of a trial. The path leads to an excellent view of the tiny cove; its white sandy bottom and blue waters are set in the frame of the red cliffs on which you stand. 🍎

San Cristobal and Nearby Sites

4

San Cristobal is getting to be much more familiar, now that its airport is being used as the arrival point for many visitors. The port, Puerto Baquerizo Moreno, is the administrative center for the Islands. A ramble down the main street can be enjoyable, and a cool drink is often welcome. Birding in the hills behind the town can be rewarding, too.

Directly south of San Cristobal is Hood Island. It is the nesting site of the waved albatross and there are colonies of masked and blue-footed boobies as well. When you land on Hood you are greeted by some of the largest and most colorful of the marine iguanas, and usually by lots of sea lions.

West of Hood is Floreana, where there's a good chance to see flamingos and migrating shorebirds in its large brackish lagoon. For human history, Post Office Bay is the place to go. It's a place that reminds you that Darwin came to this spot, and you'll see mementos of many more recent visitors.

For snorkelers, one of the best moments of the trip can be a quick visit to Devil's Crown, just a few hundred meters off Floreana. This ominous-looking, partially submerged lava cone provides a protected area for swimming. If the weather is good and the sea calm, you'll want to get into your panga for the short trip to the middle of the Crown and slip over the side for a few minutes of underwater beauty.

San Cristobal (Chatham)

San Cristobal, in the far southeast of the archipelago, has had a long, and not always pleasant, human history. It had no regular inhabitants when it was visited for five days by Darwin, in September of 1835. His first view of it (not at the comfortable cove where you will disembark) was quite intimidating.

> *Nothing could be less inviting than the first appearance. A broken field of black, basaltic lava, thrown into the most rugged waves, and crossed by great fissures, is everywhere covered by stunted, sunburnt brushwood, which shows little signs of life. The dry and parched surface, being heated by the noonday sun, gave to the air a close and sultry feeling, like that from a stove; we fancied even that the bushes smelt unpleasantly.*
> (Darwin pp. 374–375)

◀ Short-eared owl at rock fissure

What saved this particular excursion for Darwin was meeting two of the tortoises—something today's visitors are very unlikely to experience, due to the very small numbers on this island.

He reported:

The day was glowing hot, and the scramble over the rough surface and through the intricate thickets, was very fatiguing; but I was well repaid by the strange Cyclopean scene. As I was walking along I met two large tortoises, each of which must have weighed two hundred pounds: one was eating a piece of cactus, and as I approached, it stared at me and slowly stalked away; the other gave a deep hiss, and drew in its head. These huge reptiles, surrounded by the black lava, the leafless shrubs, and large cacti, seemed to my fancy like some antediluvian animals.
(Darwin pp. 375–376)

In 1841 there was a small settlement established on San Cristobal by a group of convicts who rebelled from their brutal treatment in the colony on Floreana. The history of the exploitation of convicts or laborers, and of repeated attempts to set up some form of island haven, continued into this century.

But now San Cristobal is the home of about 3000 farmers and fishing people, and is the Ecuadorean administrative headquarters for all of the Islands. There is a small naval base there as well and one of the two airstrips in the Islands.

PUERTO BAQUERIZO MORENO

For the visitor there is the opportunity to stroll around the town of Puerto Baquerizo Moreno, pass by the statue of Darwin, go into a local cafe for a cool drink and check out the small museum and the shops there. It may be that your guide will arrange for the group to take a bus to the highlands and the small lake, El Junco.

Now that San Cristobal has an airport and a number of tours start and end there, the town is undergoing some rapid enhancement, in terms of the quality of tourist-related facilities. It's a good place for a swim or a beer in a local cantina.

EL JUNCO LAGOON

This whole round trip is an easy one, and will be in total only two to three hours, depending on how much time the group takes enjoying the birding and the view.

This small freshwater lake is an excellent place for birding, and the trip up to it takes you through several vegetation zones. You reach the lake by bus, which will have to be arranged by your captain or guide, and you will pass into the more humid levels of the island, where farming takes place.

Yellow warbler *(Dendroica petechai)*

The view of the lake itself is lovely, and the birding is a wonderful mixture of shorebirds, drawn by the fresh water, and of the island's distinctive land birds. At the lake there can be whimbrels, stilts, white-cheeked pintail ducks and common gallinules.

As for land birds, seven of the Darwin's finches are listed as being here. Telling one from another is a challenge. You might be particularly lucky and see a warbler finch here, with its tiny thin bill. It's hard to believe it is actually a finch.

Puerto Baquerizo Moreno is also the jumping-off point for several small excursions to nearby islands. Isla Colon offers a dry landing, sea lions and frigate birds. And Kicker Rock and Isla Lobos are impressive sites, often visited on the last afternoon before the departure from the airport at the village.

Floreana (Santa Maria, Charles)

Floreana is located at the southern edge of the archipelago, and almost exactly at the center of its east/west dimension. It is about a five-hour trip from the south coast of Santa Cruz, or from Espanola (Hood) to its east.

There are three visitor sites: Punta Cormoran, with its flamingo lagoon and its two lovely beaches; Post Office Bay, still the place to send mail to friends around the world; and a lava tube that can be followed far underground.

Just northwest of Punta Cormoran is Devil's Crown, an excellent diving site, which is usually reached from your Punta Cormoran anchorage.

PUNTA CORMORAN

Punta Cormoran is a steep, not-very-large lava cone on a point of land joined to the larger island by a low-lying strip of vegetated dune. You approach the site by a wet landing in a pleasant cove. The beach sand itself is of interest because it has a considerable proportion of olivine crystals, derived from volcanic action, which have a pale olive color.

You move up the usual beach slope, passing though the dune vegetation. Shortly, the trail ascends slightly along a hill that faces the Punta cone itself. At the high point of the trail, only a few minutes from the start, you look down into a large lagoon. Its water level varies greatly — from mostly mud flats to to nearly a lake (in the El Nino year). At any time, it is likely to be an excellent place for bird-watching. Flamingos are common. From this height you may see the underwater trails that they make through the mud as they sieve through the turbid water to extract minute crustaceans. At first you may think the lines are the traces of cracks that were formed in the mud when it was very dry; but then as you follow a flamingo's movements you see that these curving, wobbling lines are made by them.

The edges of the lagoon, particularly on the northwest side, have vegetation right to the water, and are good for spotting shorebirds. We saw a phalarope (no one could decide which species), a willet, and white-cheeked pintail ducks. Whimbrels, semi-palmated plovers, and wandering tattlers are regularly seen there in small numbers, too.

Don't forget to look at the bird life right around you at the viewpoint. I had an excellent look at the Galapagos large-billed flycatcher, complete with an insect gripped in its beak. There are a variety of the finches, with small and medium ground finches and the cactus finch listed as "abundant" in the bird guide.

After your pause at the viewpoint, you will go about 350 meters farther to one of the most perfect beaches in the Islands. It lines a shallow cove, with the finest of white sands. It is like granulated sugar. And populating the sand are multitudes of ghost crabs. They hide from your approach and then come up from their tiny holes to skitter down the beach in search of food. You'll be lucky to see them, between their shyness and

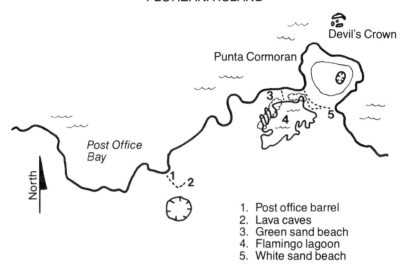

FLOREANA ISLAND

Devil's Crown

Punta Cormoran

Post Office
Bay

North

1. Post office barrel
2. Lava caves
3. Green sand beach
4. Flamingo lagoon
5. White sand beach

the difficulty of picking out their pale, translucent bodies, even when they are above ground.

Once when we were at this beach, it was visited by a number of rays—probably stingrays—which were about a meter across. They came right up to the water's edge, just skimming along well within view.

We swam here once, in the El Nino year, when the water was about 25 degrees C., and it remains one of our best memories. The ground falls away very gradually, and there were no waves or currents. It was like our own private pool, just right for gently stroking from one side of the cove to the other, or for standing quietly up to your neck and watching the light change on the Palo Santo that clothe Floreana's graceful slopes.

POST OFFICE BAY

Post Office Bay is just a short boat ride to the west of Punta Cormoran. You land on a brown beach, perhaps sharing it with a few sea lions, and walk beyond the beach a couple of minutes to a small clearing in the scrub. This is not a prepossessing place. It looks very tired and worn, with few redeeming features. But you are here for its human history, for that big wooden barrel that still holds mail for the world.

The barrel itself is covered with signs from boats that have visited over the years. People seem to have made the signs themselves, raiding wooden slats from driftwood, or even using plaques that have their boat

name carved in them! It is interesting to see the variety of names and places from which they came. And it's completely contained, right on the barrel and its little pedestal, so it's the only acceptable graffiti in the Islands.

There are still seven families that live on this island, about 30 people in all. There is even a tiny tea shop there, at Black Beach. Marguerite Wittmer, who came here in the 1930s, runs it and also supervises the post office barrel. Visitors love to send mail via this method. Guides will open the little door and pull out a handful of envelopes. They check for letters that other visitors want sent. If one goes to your country, then you take it along, stamp it when you get there, and off it goes. You might even attach a note telling the addressee when you picked it up. We sent some off as soon as we got to our home airport, and the ones that we had deposited in the barrel were delivered before we got home ourselves, so it's pretty effective.

THE LAVA TUBE

This lava tube is harder to actually enter than the ones in the High-lands of Santa Cruz. It starts out as a hole in the flat ground about 10 minutes' walk past the post office barrel. Your guide will have a rope to help you rappel down a rope in mountaineer fashion for the five meters or so to the first level spot.

According to my nephew Cricket, the entrance is straight down, and then there's a descending, low-ceilinged shaft down to the floor. They walked a few minutes along the smooth bottom until encountering water. They then took off their shoes and continued on through the deepening water, continuing forward minus shorts and shirts, finally having to swim to reach the end of the cave.

This whole little excursion to the tube end and back was about an hour in length.

Other Islands: Devil's Crown, Hood

DEVIL'S CROWN

Devil's Crown, also called Onslow Island, is a small but very exciting place to visit. It is located just 250 meters from Floreana's shore, a few minutes' panga-ride from the Punta Cormoran anchorage. Your boat will probably stay there and send you over in groups of four to the site itself. Devil's Crown is the partially exposed cone of an extinct volcano. Its once-complete circle of rock has been broken in several places, allowing the sea to come in. Its black sides are so steep, so craggy and harsh-looking, that it's easy to see how it could acquire this sinister name.

The walls are splashed at the top with the whitewash of bird excre-ment, and the only thing that seems to grow there are two kinds of cactus

◄ Descending into the lava tube

(*Jasminocereus thouarsii*, the candelabra cactus, and *Opuntia megasperma*, the prickly pear). But birds love the place, and you can see red-billed tropic birds, pelicans, lava gulls, and frigate birds sitting on the jagged rocks, loafing or waiting for the right time to go out to feed. Even the occasional heron will be seen there. Your captain will be glad to circle the island a couple of times so you can get a good look.

But if you get a chance to go snorkeling in the center of the Crown, you will be very glad you did. The panga will be tethered to a line that is in turn attached to a big concrete block at the western side of the inner circle. (This is to prevent descending anchors from destroying the rich life that clings to the rocks and strews the ocean floor.)

While the currents outside the Crown can be fierce, and the surrounding sea is known as a good place for shark-watching, the inside is a calm, non-threatening place. You will always be near your panga, and you can rest awhile on the tiny beach that is exposed at low tide. And the underwater life is dream-like in its beauty and variety. From huge sea lions whipping past you to layer upon layer of different species of fish to the sea stars and tube corals and sea cucumbers on the bottom, there is enough to occupy you for hours. (My favorites were the schools of needlefish that hung by the hundreds right at the top of the water, gleaming in the light from above). The cold of the water will probably force you out long before your interest has waned.

Even if you aren't much of a swimmer, and hate cold water, do try to snorkel here (assuming it is a calm enough day that the captain feels it would be safe for all). I found myself quite uneasy here on my last trip, because of the cold water, so I held on to the captain's hand and we paddled lazily along, he the courteous gentleman as always. Just ask for a "buddy" and you'll have one instantly.

HOOD (ESPANOLA)

Hood is a fairly flat island, rising slightly from sea level on its north side to rugged black cliffs perhaps 30 meters high on its south side. The landing there is one of the more exciting you will have, because the boat has to anchor about 200 meters or more out to sea. Then the panga has to take a rather circuitous route over barely submerged rocks, through real ocean waves, to get to the sheltered calm of its landing place. Extra caution with the cameras is called for here; keep them well-protected.

Once you land you are immediately in the midst of such numbers and variety of wildlife that it is almost too much to absorb. There are likely to be many sea lions, both in the little cove and right on shore where you disembark. Then within a few steps you see dozens, even hundreds of marine iguanas on the rocks at the back edge of the sandy beach.

These iguanas are not like any others in the Islands. They are the same species, but the Hood race is very distinct for its having the largest average size of all marine iguanas and for its quite striking coloring. It has

PUNTA SUAREZ, HOOD ISLAND

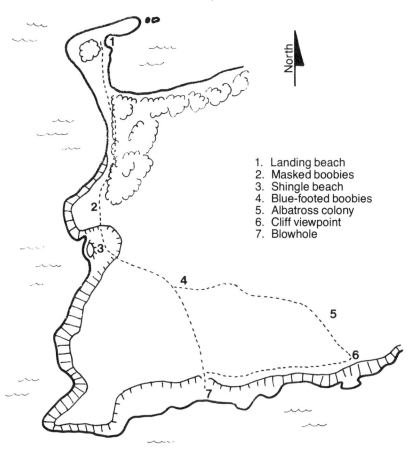

North

1. Landing beach
2. Masked boobies
3. Shingle beach
4. Blue-footed boobies
5. Albatross colony
6. Cliff viewpoint
7. Blowhole

patches of dark red on its sides, a greenish tinge along its ridged back and the usual black everywhere else.

If you see lava lizards, these are a species unique to Hood (*Tropidurus delanonis*). These are the largest lava lizards in the Islands; they are also notable for having the shortest, thickest tail. The female has red under her chin and at the base of her tail. The male is rather speckled—black, yellow and green.

Within just a few more steps you will reach the first approach to a cliff edge, where you will see a nesting area for masked boobies. They have a yearly breeding cycle, starting in November with egg-laying and ending in June when the young are able to fly and feed on their own. Next you will

Blowhole at cliff base on Hood Island

descend for a few meters to a small shingle beach and then go back up to the open expanses of low scrub and open areas that cover the island.

Your next treat is a large nesting area for blue-footed boobies. They do not have the distinctively defined breeding season of the masked boobies, and you may see eggs or any stage of development in the young at any time of year.

The beautiful Galapagos dove will be pecking and probing on the ground here and there. They seem less wary of people here than they do on other islands. Completely unwary and, in fact, very aggressive, is the Hood mockingbird (*Nesomimus macdonaldi*), which is found only here and on a nearby rocky islet, Gardner-near-Hood. It is somewhat larger than the other three species of mockingbird found on the Islands, and it has a heavier, more down-curved beak. It has hazel-colored eyes. And you will get close enough to see the color of those eyes, because these mockers are nearly pestiferous in their approach to people. They hop on your shoes, sit on your hat, jump on your packsack. You can get the most "touristy" of pictures, without trying in any way to lure them to you. They come whether you like it or not.

The bushes should be scanned for the large-billed race of the large cactus finch (*Geospiza conirostris*) and a very gray sub-species of the warbler finch (*Certhidea olivacea*). The small ground finch (*Geospiza fuliginosa*) nests on the island and so does the large-billed flycatcher.

Then, only about 400 meters from the beginning of the trail, you will come to the only place where the waved albatross nests (with the exception of a few pairs which nest on a tiny island off the coast of Ecuador). The

12,000 pairs that nest yearly on Hood are, effectively, the entire population of this bird in the world. For the nature-lover there is something quite moving about being able to be within a few meters of all the varied activity that goes on as these birds lay their eggs and care for their young.

The setting, too, is quite dramatic, for you are near the edge of high, black cliffs, with the waves far below rolling in from the open sea to the east. There are many kinds of sea birds sitting next to you on the rocks, and others soaring above and below you. And every few minutes, especially in the early morning, a huge albatross waddles to the edge of the cliff, makes a few awkward wing flaps and then launches itself out on the updrafts to become one of the world's most graceful and efficient soaring beings.

Depending on when you are there, you may see a great deal of the elaborate display these birds make as they claim and maintain territory, or as they form their pairs and trade off the care of their young at the nest. (They mate for life; so only birds mating for their first time, at four or five years of age, will be doing the pair-formation or courtship displays to any great degree. However, toward the end of the breeding season, already-established pairs will do displays like this as they consolidate their relationship for the year to come.)

There are several detailed descriptions of the displays in the scientific literature (see Suggested Reading), but to the uninitiated, the central theme of the courtship movement seems to be variations on "fencing." The birds cross bills, click them, throw their heads high and make loud honking noises and then resume the thrust and dodge of their bills. It's noisy, and exciting to watch. Part of the display is a vast exaggeration of their ordinary rolling walk, a gait that makes them look like the most drunken and macho sailor just hitting dry land after months at sea in a very small boat.

The overall breeding season of this albatross is from the end of March through December, with August to December being the most active times. To see the huge eggs, the adorably ugly chicks, the waddling adults that turn into incomparably fine flyers after they project themselves off the edge of the cliffs, is to participate in one of the premier privileges of visiting the Galapagos.

On your way back from the albatross grounds you may descend the cliffs nearby to the blowhole that shoots a plume of spray 15 to 30 meters in the air. There is a crevice at sea level where the surging water rushes in and is then almost trapped except for this one upward exit. The spume is impressive, and fun to dart in and out of.

Also on the way back, along the rocks at sea level, there are tide pools frequented by sea lions. It is a good place to photograph them in very clear, calm water. The shore is also good for shorebirds like the oystercatcher, a few of which breed on Hood. The rocky cliffs are nesting places for the swallow-tailed gull, the red-billed tropic bird and Audubon's shearwater. 🍎

Isabela and Nearby Sites 5

I sabela and Fernandina seem more rugged and inaccessible than the other islands of the Galapagos, partly because a number of the visitor sites are many hours by boat from the central core of Santa Cruz and Santiago. Not all itineraries can include visits to the west side of Isabela because of the limitations brought on by time, weather and sea. A trip to Urbina Bay to see its recently uplifted coral beds, or to Punta Espinoza on Fernandina, involve long and tiring trips on seas that are rarely calm. But you are likely to have one good chance to land on Isabela's east side, for a short visit to Punta Garcia, where you take the panga to a nesting site of flightless cormorants. And if your group is up for it, you may get a chance to do the one-day trek up Volcan Alcedo, just above the waist of Isabela.

In any case, you will often see Alcedo or other looming volcanos as your trip takes you between the island and Santiago or Santa Cruz.

Isabela (Albemarle)

I sabela is the largest of all the islands of the Galapagos. It is on the west side of the archipelago and is over 100 kilometers long, but relatively narrow. Its most narrow point, the Perry Isthmus, is about one-third up from the southern edge of the island.

Isabela has the most imposing terrain in the Islands, composed as it is of six towering shield volcanoes that have merged over the millennia, forming the mountainous profile seen today. Two of the six volcanoes (Wolf and Cerro Azul) are over 1700 meters high. The one that is most likely to be visited, Alcedo, is about 1200 meters high—high enough for a challenging hike and a very satisfying view.

Because Isabela is rather far from the central islands of the archipelago, and because the trip to its far side is very time-consuming and can at times be very rough, most visitors will be fortunate to be able to visit one particular site — Punta Garcia, to see the flightless cormorants. However, if your trip is a two-week one and your boat is fast, at least one or two of the other visitor areas will be possible.

PUNTA GARCIA

Punta Garcia is a small outcropping, mostly of a-a (pronounced ah-ah)

◀ Penguin on cliffs at Tagus Cove

lava. The boat will anchor in a very small and rather exposed cove a few minutes' panga-ride from the visitor site itself.

The little cove has some interest of its own if your crew can take you on a short panga trip skirting along the low, ragged shoreline. There are some mangroves along the edge and you may see some lava herons fishing along there.

Also of interest is how the crew have to anchor the boat to keep it from coming to harm. Punta Garcia is not in a very protected area and each time I've been there the seas were quite rough. The smallness and shallowness of the anchorage, combined with the turbulence of the water just a few meters away, means that the crew has to put out two or even three anchor points. First, they drop one anchor and then move the boat as far away from it as the chain will allow. Then they attach a rope to the other end of the boat and take its loose end and go out in the panga. They take the free end of the rope to shore and attach it to the sturdiest-looking branch, tethering the boat from end to end, and keeping it from bashing into the rocky shore. On one particularly rough trip I was on, the crew let out two anchors — from the bow and the port stern—and then they tied us up with a third line to shore, not taking any chances.

Then the fun really begins for the visitor — the brief (five minutes) panga-ride to the flightless cormorants area. The ride is directly against the waves, and there is a lot of splashing and bouncing up and down (be sure to have your cameras completely protected in plastic bags). There are usually a few morbid jokes about how you couldn't swim to the shore if the panga went over because the lava is so rough you'd just bleed to death if you tried to climb up on it. But the boatman knows a lot more about the limits of the boat than most visitors do; trust and a few unspoken prayers will get you there. However, boats actually have sunk on this little junket, and it would be foolish not to wear your life jacket. Non-swimmers might want to forgo this visit unless the sea is completely calm — not a likely event.

In another very small cove, the boatman's helper will jump out first to assist everyone off the boat. The help is required to make sure no one slips and falls on the lava. A-a is the proper name for it, but the Spanish name, scoria, is far more expressive—it means "garbage." And the surface does look like some monster regurgitated black bile from the depths of the water, and then everything was just frozen in time and space.

The first few steps are spent just stepping along extremely carefully to avoid the humps and cracks. The "land" is barely above water level, so there is no steepness or crevasses—just enough variation to turn an ankle or take a fall. If you do, it's like landing on a bed of glass shards. It's not frightening; it's mostly impressive that a field of rock could be so dramatic.

Then, as you first tear your eyes away from your feet and you look ahead a very few meters, there are the flightless cormorants! Actually, the first thing you'll see will be swaths of white—the whitewash of bird guano around the birds' nests. The dark brown birds, nearly black when wet, blend in very well with the black background — so much so that on one of

Flightless cormorants at nest

my visits we had to grab one of the visitors before she accidentally stepped on a bird!

At Punta Garcia there are likely to be only three or four nests—this is a small outpost of breeding birds. But you will be able to see them sitting on their nests, perhaps with a fluffy, reptilian-looking young one peeking out from beneath the parent's chest. Others may be standing in their characteristic spread-wing posture, which they adopt to dry their water-soaked wings. (Like all cormorants and their allies they do not have a great deal of oil for waterproofing their wings, so they must hang themselves out to dry after a fishing expedition.) When they are doing this you will see very well how short and sparse their wings are, obviously of no possible assistance in flight. If you can see one underwater as it approaches the rocks, you'll see the role its wings play in swimming.

Another fascinating thing about these cormorants is the color of their eyes. When the light is on them, the eyes are a most luminous aquamarine blue. There is little depth to them and just the tiniest pupil, but the combination of the brilliance and yet almost opaque quality of the color makes a most intriguing picture.

And speaking of pictures, photographing here is particularly demanding. It seems, first of all, that you are likely to arrive near the end of a day— that was true in three trips for me, anyway. So the light will be very low, and fading quickly. Then you will have dull black rocks as the overall background, big splashes of bright white guano right against the birds, and the dark birds themselves. It is very important to be familiar with any mechanisms your camera has for compensating for extremely high contrast situations between subject and background. Underexpose by one or two stops, and "bracket" your shots (i.e., take each one of them by turns under-exposed, exactly exposed, and over-exposed, according to your meter).

These are special birds and you will have come far to see them, so you won't want to lose a chance by not knowing your camera well. But also watch closely that you do not agitate the birds, even if it means not staying too long and perhaps not getting a history-making shot. Finally, wear long pants, because kneeling even gingerly on the abrasive lava can scratch or cut your bare skin.

VOLCAN ALCEDO

Volcan Alcedo sits at mid-point of the island. It can be reached from its eastern side, from a disembarkation point at Shipton Cove. This hike can be a high point of any trip, but to do it you must arrange **before** you leave home to take a two-night camping trip there. Your travel agent should be able to ask for this and have it confirmed before you leave. (If your travel agent cannot help you, look for another agent who can.) These camping trips are booked only into an overall trip length of **two weeks.**

The captain of a boat has to get permission from the Park and the Darwin Station to take a group overnight, and he has to be sure it will fit in with the overall itinerary, etc. If you are camping, you will want to bring very lightweight camping equipment. Rain gear, water bottles, first-aid kit, sleeping bag, ground sheet, etc., are all necessary if you stay overnight.

It is possible to do a one-day round trip up Alcedo (as I did), but it is not the optimal way to see this dramatic place. For a day trip, as with the hike up Sugarloaf, your captain and the guide will make an informal assessment of the group's interests and fitness and will then suggest—or refrain from suggesting—that the trip be attempted. Talk it over and see what you and they come up with. Of course, the overall trip schedule, weather conditions, etc., will be big factors in the final decision. And even if you have confirmed the camping trip from home, do remember that sudden changes in weather, currents, etc., can cancel the camping trip entirely. It's all a part of this kind of "adventure" travel.

You must be prepared for a 20-kilometer (round trip) hike that can take the powerful hiker less than three hours (one way), but will easily take five or six hours for the less athletic. Wear lightweight hiking boots or very sturdy running shoes, with two pairs of socks to avoid blisters. Do what you can to keep the fine grit along the trail from getting into your shoes and causing abrasions. And bring as much water as possible, even if it means more weight. You'll be very glad you did. You'll want to have an early start if you're doing it in one day, or even if your group has permission for the longer trip.

But if you do go, you have a real adventure in store. On my own one-day trip, the first half of the time on the trail up was spent on an easy, gradual ascent through the changing vegetative zones, on a wide, smooth trail, which parallels an a-a lava flow. First you travel through the sparse vegetation of the arid zone and then move into the transition zone with its scattered trees, some with patches of moss hanging here and there. The finches are common, and I had an excellent view of the warbler finch. There were several large-billed flycatchers, quite oblivious to me and my camera, and some vermilion flycatchers. As the trail reaches the cone itself the route becomes decidedly more taxing. The slope is steep and the footing isn't very solid. It has a rough, granular quality, and is crumbling from overuse. You are roughly at the half-way point of the climb (i.e., if you've been two hours on the trail, expect another two hours for this last short distance). It's a real scramble, sometimes on hands and knees and sometimes depending on plant handholds to keep going.

At the top you come out on a fairly flat area, with lots of small trees and scrub brush. The view back along the trail to the cove and on to Santiago in the distance is spectacular. The varying results of the sculpting of vulcanism on Isabela and the other islands is very clear. There is a beautiful contrast in colors, from the khaki of the hills to the pale water edge, then

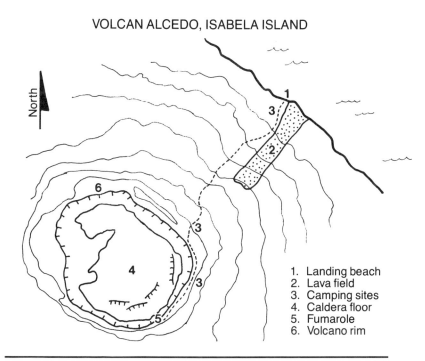

VOLCAN ALCEDO, ISABELA ISLAND

North

1. Landing beach
2. Lava field
3. Camping sites
4. Caldera floor
5. Fumarole
6. Volcano rim

the brilliant turquoise of the shallower water and the deeper blues and then steel-gray of the open ocean. You'll be proud of how far you've come.

You'll be standing near the edge of the crater, the sunken center of the volcano. On some days you can see wisps of steam coming from a fumarole six kilometers away on the south side of the crater wall. It is hard to grasp the size of the cone upon which you are standing. (The diameter is seven kilometers at its widest.) You can take little sorties along the rim; there are paths going in either direction. But probably your group will sit and eat lunch in what little shade there is. All too soon, it will be time to go back.

Keep an eye out for the tortoises that shuffle through the bush. As with each of Isabela's dominant volcanic cones, Alcedo has its own distinct race. We saw just one, quite small, but exciting to see nonetheless. If you're lucky and it has rained recently, you might come across a rain puddle that is being visited by the tortoises for drinking and wallowing. January seems to be a particularly good month to see them in great numbers. We also saw a wild donkey, an unpleasant reminder of the ongoing struggle for the scarce food resources of the island. According to my nephew Skeeter, "The sight of a burro reminds you of a docile, tame creature pulling a cart or grazing in a field. But this wild beast which bolted at the sight of us was totally different."

After the hike back, you will be very glad to take a quick dip in the little cove. You probably will want to go in with all your grimy, sweat-soaked clothes on, just to cool down and clean off. It's a real treat.

At the campsite at Volcan Alcedo

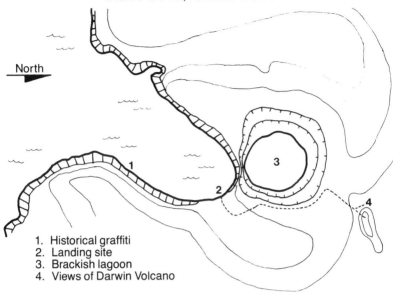

TAGUS COVE, ISABELA ISLAND

North

1. Historical graffiti
2. Landing site
3. Brackish lagoon
4. Views of Darwin Volcano

TAGUS COVE

Tagus Cove is a seldom-visited site on the northwest side of Isabela. There are two activities for the visitor, one on land and the other on water. The land trip is a short walk up to Darwin Lake, which is a salt-water lagoon that is actually above sea level. The slopes are clothed with typical arid zone vegetation. The chief draws of the visit are a good selection of birds, getting a good view of a crater lake and views of Darwin and Wolf volcanoes.

Upon landing, you may find a couple of flightless cormorant nests. When on the trail, there will probably be a variety of finches, possibly even the woodpecker finch. There may be mockingbirds and even evidence of tortoises, if not the beasts themselves. This also is often a great area for seeing the Galapagos hawk.

The cliffs that enfold the bay are marred by extensive graffiti, put there by crews and passengers of many of the ships that have come here over the years. The ones that are very old have some historical interest, but fortunately this practice has been sufficiently discouraged that it has become virtually extinct.

The other activity for visitors is a ride in the panga along the cliffs. There are shelves of rock near the entrance of the cove and here you may see a few Galapagos penguins and flightless cormorants. Blue-footed boobies are likely, and there may be marine iguanas. The panga ride is a very pleasant way to see the sea-based wildlife from another perspective, though it can be difficult to photograph from the gently rocking boat.

Uplifted coral—now rock in a field

URBINA BAY

Urbina Bay is also on the west coast of Isabela, directly west of Volcan Alcedo. There is an easy wet landing to a gently sloping beach and then what looks to be just another scrubby plain stretching out beyond. But this area is extremely interesting because it has a dramatic and beautiful example of the geological activity of the Islands: in 1954, five kilometers of the marine reef at the edge of the shore were uplifted four meters!

No one was there at the time, but not too long afterwards a Disney film crew was sailing in the area and they noticed that the beach area gleamed unusually white. As they got closer, they saw that this whiteness was due to conglomerates of coral and calcium-based algae that were totally out of their watery element! And on these uplifted rocks were stranded sea animals—lobsters, marine turtles and even fish, in the pools in the pitted surface. Obviously, if these active animals had gotten trapped like that, the whole event must have happened very quickly.

Exactly why it happened is not clear, but the likelihood is that some subterranean shift of molten lava, perhaps due to volcanic activity on Alcedo or the more southern Sierra Negra, was responsible for this movement of the earth's crust.

For today's visitor, it can be a very odd sensation to walk on dry land right in the middle of a bed of coral, with large "boulders" of it almost waist-high. (The globular coral, curiously brain-like in surface texture, is now a dull black in color.) It is also a beautiful place, with the clumps of coral with their intricate surfaces, and the remnants of barnacles, sea shells, sea worms and other creatures embedded in them, or strewn here and there on the ground.

Fernandina (Narborough)

Fernandina, the farthest west of the Galapagos Islands, is one of the most volcanically active in the archipelago. Because of its distance from the center of the Islands, and because it is a particularly lengthy trip to reach it, this island is visited relatively rarely by touring groups. It is an intriguing place, and well worth the trip, if it can be managed.

Fernandina is about 1500 meters high, with its main crater being about 6.5 kilometers wide. It is one of the most recent of the islands. It does not have the rich floral life that some of the other islands of its height display, partly because so much of it has been coated with recent lava flows and inundations of volcanic ash, and partly because Isabela's heights "capture" much of the rain it might get from moist air coming from the east.

Fernandina's volcano has erupted several times in this century. In 1968 it erupted and the floor of its crater, already 610 meters below its rim, dropped another few hundred meters. In 1977 the volcano erupted again, sending rivers of lava into its lake from a crack in the crater wall. Then the following year another eruption occurred, with more lava spewed into the crater. But for the ordinary visitor will see only the outside slopes of this crater, along with sweeps of black lava from flows that happened before our time.

PUNTA ESPINOZA

The landing site itself is on a spit of black lava rock, reminiscent of the recent flows of Sullivan Bay. The landing is a dry one, in a tiny, mangrove-lined inlet. Sometimes there are many marine iguanas right at the landing site, on the rocks. The trail goes in two directions, to the left to a field of a-a lava, and to the right to the "land's end." I was able to visit only the area to the right.

The point itself has rich and varied wildlife, even if the surroundings are stark and barren, except for the small patches of mangrove where you land. In ordinary times there are nesting flightless cormorants and penguins, and a number of marine iguanas perched on the rocks and on bits of driftwood stuck in the cracks in the lava.

I was there in an El Nino year, and there seemed to be an ominous quality to the whole point. There was but one flightless cormorant to be seen and the distressing sight of a lone sea lion pup, its ribs showing through its fur, leaning against a piece of driftwood, seemingly with not long to live. (Few young ones did that year.) It was late in the afternoon, and we'd had an exhausting voyage to this place. It all seemed a dull monochrome—gray sky, black rocks, gray spines of driftwood, dark iguanas,

PUNTA ESPINOZA, FERNANDINA ISLAND

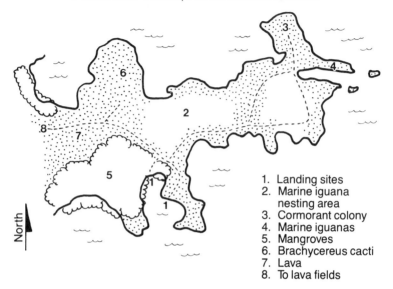

1. Landing sites
2. Marine iguana nesting area
3. Cormorant colony
4. Marine iguanas
5. Mangroves
6. Brachycereus cacti
7. Lava
8. To lava fields

North

dully colored sea lion pup. We all felt very gray ourselves and hoped to come back the next day to spend more time and exorcise our depression, but heavy seas prevented it.

But your own visit will undoubtedly have its own character, most likely the more usual exciting and uplifting one. If you have a chance to examine the mangrove area, there should be a variety of herons. Yellow warblers and mockingbirds are found here, too. The great blue herons and some pelicans nest here. The birding guide says that the Galapagos rail and mangrove finch have been reported here in the past, but not recently. The shore area is a good place to look for migrant shorebirds and for petrels, shearwaters and frigate birds. The Audubon's shearwaters apparently fly inland at night to roost in the crevices of the broken lava fields. And the frigate birds sleep in the mangroves. If the sea is calm, snorkeling is good along the point, with a real chance of seeing marine iguanas feeding alongside you underwater. 🐢

Motor sailer for small group tours in James Bay ▶

PART III. *Travel Tips*

Are The Islands For You? 1

The Galapagos Islands are a very special place — but not a destination suitable to every traveler. Part II of this book has taken you as a visitor to most of the sites where you are likely to go. That will have told you some things about the pleasures and rigors of such a trip, but the following material is written specifically to help you decide if you are a likely candidate for this adventure, considering the kind and amount of travel involved, the living conditions, approximate cost of a trip and the physical and mental requirements. At the end of this section there will be a brief consideration of travel in mainland Ecuador. And finally, for those who are getting ready to go, there will be a list of things to bring with you, and a section of tips for photographing in these demanding conditions. 🐢

Swimming at the fur seal grottos, Santiago Island

Planning a Visit

2

The Galapagos wildlife is very free, but the visitors are a highly controlled element of the environment. You may visit the Park segments only in a registered and licensed boat and only with a trained guide. The boats are almost exclusively available through travel agents and tour operators who sub-contract the services described in their brochures and trip plans. It is often difficult, and quite unnecessary, to make direct arrangements with boat owner/operators on your own, unless you happen to know one personally.

Making Arrangements

Though you should go through a travel agent or tour, you have some real choices with either kind of arrangement. It is entirely possible to book your own flights, through a travel agent or on your own with the airline, to Quito and the Islands. You can minimize costs by booking your own flights, and having your travel agent book hotels in Quito or Miami (the usual jumping-off place), but this can mean a little more uncertainty if your hotel in Ecuador has lost your booking or you are not comfortable taking taxis out of airports where they do not speak a lot of English. I've done it both ways and there are advantages and glitches with each. It is the actual boat time that must be booked through an agent. If you go on a tour, perhaps with a birding group or your local natural history museum, it is likely that this tour will include all the bookings of flights and accommodation on the way, as well as the boat time in the Islands.

Current (January, 1989) costs of airfares in U.S. dollars for Miami/Quito/Galapagos and return are the following:

        SAETA (Ecuadorian ownership):
            low season $560
            high season $630
        Ecuatoriana:
            low season $659
            high season $730
        Eastern Airlines (U.S.)
            low season $720
            high season over $800

And: Ecuatoriana: *Los Angeles*/Quito/Galapagos: $899

It is best to book the three-part flight all at once if you are doing it yourself, because the round-trip flight from Quito to the Islands, if booked separately, is $367 U.S. When you are pricing tours, it might be a good idea to compare these costs and the average costs per night on the various boats, to see whether you think a particular arrangement is acceptably priced for you. Also, visitors from the United Kingdom probably can keep their costs down by booking some of the extremely low fares to Canada, and then carrying on their trip from there.

There is a very wide range of prices and types of boats to choose from through standard traveling channels. So, do one or all of the following: see your travel agent, call the Ecuadorean consul nearest you for any information they have, check your favorite nature magazine for advertisements of tour companies, and talk with friends. You probably won't have to go far to find someone who has made the trip, or at least knows someone who has.

Planning the length of a visit

First, the trip to the Islands is a long one from almost anywhere, even for Ecuadoreans who fly or sail the 1000 kilometers from the mainland to get there. From just about anywhere in the United States or Canada, you should expect a full day's travel to reach Quito. When scheduling your trip, it is absolutely essential that you allow yourself *at least* 24 hours in Quito before the planned departure for the Islands themselves. This trip in itself can be very tiring; also, Quito is over 3000 meters in altitude, so it is common for people to suffer somewhat from the thin air. (Just take it easy, don't rush about, rest often.)

The conditions in Quito are relevant to travelers; I strongly recommend that visitors spend at least a week in mainland Ecuador, with several of those days in Quito and the surrounding mountains.

It is possible to visit the Galapagos for as little as three nights—if you take the large cruise boats that fly in their passengers from Quito or Guayaquil, on the coast of Ecuador. (These boats are called the *Santa Cruz*, *Galapagos Explorer* and the *Buccaneer*.) This option is my least-favored one. In this mode of travel you can visit only a limited number of sites, because the large number of people on these cruise ships causes too much wear and tear on sites and therefore the ships are not allowed to visit widely. Also, you are always in groups of at least 25. Sometimes all 90 people are taken to a site at once! It is a crowd scene and not conducive to the more leisurely and much more personalized experience made possible by the small boat offerings.

You can also book trips of 7, 14 or even 21 nights. A seven-night tour can be done on the *Isabela II*, a 34-passenger luxury yacht. It has a very comprehensive itinerary even in this relatively short time because it travels at 12.5 knots and has full navigational equipment. This equipment means it can travel at night or in fog, which not all boats are equipped to do. The visitors are divided into groups of 17 each for the on-shore visits.

Small-tour motor sailer at anchor, Santa Fe Island

The other boats also book for seven nights, and a number of them offer 14- and 21-night visits as well. These boats are smaller than the *Isabela II,* and they offer a range of comfort levels and prices. (Always remember that the same boat may have one price for one tour group or travel agent and another price for a different one. This all depends on the business practices of the agent or tour business. So do compare!) These smaller boats carry between 6 and 16 people. A few of them are motor/ sailers, which adds another element of adventure to the trip (and a calmer ride, with the sails up). To my mind, the ideal trip should be for two weeks, on one of these much smaller boats. The reasoning for this is based on a combination of factors such as costs, completeness of Island coverage and overall ambience of a trip taken in the small-boat conditions.

The Galapagos cover a lot of territory. These smaller boats travel from 5 to 8 knots, depending on size and power source (engines only, or engine and sail). These are not speed boats and there is no reason that they should be. Therefore, it will take a two-week trip to have a chance to see a wide range of sites, with all their varied plant and animal life. Two weeks is good for developing some sense of closeness to the Islands, some aware-ness of the interplay between land and water. In one week you may never see a porpoise "surfing" on the waves curling from your boat's bow—in two weeks you probably will. In one week you won't have to deal with dirty clothes or fussy shipmates. In two weeks you'll be happily sloshing your mildewed clothes in a bucket full of sea water and shampoo/sea soap. By the end of the two weeks you'll feel like you've made some life-long friends, and you'll know that one week *more* and you'd have happily pushed so-and-so overboard. To me, that's all an essential part of "adventure travel."

The three-week trips are for the most highly motivated and hardy visitors, who already know they can tolerate fairly long periods of being tossed by waves and confined in close proximity to others. The larger and more luxurious of the small boats do have enough space to get away from people at the far end of the deck. They have private bathrooms and enough storage space to keep your stuff out of the way. So, do three weeks if it seems to fit, and if you have the time. But don't leave out the possibility of using some of your hard-earned vacation time in mainland Ecuador, as well.

If your time or physical capacity is severely limited, then by all means take the seven-day option. Also, if you have young children along, seven days is probably the comfort limit for all concerned.

Time of Year for Visiting

You will find a great deal to see at most times of the year in the Galapagos. However, there are a few general guidelines to keep in mind. The busiest times for bookings are December to March and July and August. So book early for these times. In September many of the boats are in dry dock and the guides are often on refresher courses, so there will be fewer boats to choose from at that time.

As for weather, in very general terms, the mildest and driest times are February to June. Seas are calmer, days are bright without being unbearably hot on land (on the water, in the moving boat, heat is rarely a problem).

Rain is not often a disruptive factor—unless you are in the midst of an El Nino event, when rain can be very heavy at times. The El Nino current sweeps down to the Islands only every seven years on average, and does not last the whole year, so it is virtually impossible to plan around it. Just book for when you want to go and take your chances. I've been there during one of these events and it had its own fascination. ❦

Trip Cost and Living Conditions on the Boat

3

There is a pool of some 30 boats that are licensed to operate in the Islands, and virtually all travel agents and tours around the world draw on this pool, which has a total maximum carrying capacity of about 25,000 people per year. The boats named are, at the time of writing, considered by our travel agent contacts to be consistently good, at whichever level of service they offer. They are clean, have good guides and cooks, and are a good value for the money. Things change quickly in the Islands, so specific boats can't be recommended, but these names will give you some clues. The important thing is to ask around among your friends, or see if your travel agent or tour guide has been to the Islands recently, and find out which boat they were on. And don't worry if you get a boat not mentioned here; just do your research, read your brochures carefully, and you still are very likely to have a wonderful time.

In terms of cost and the luxury level of the boats, the degree of luxury from boat to boat does vary considerably, from the strictly utilitarian to the fantastically fancy. However, do keep in mind that prices for the same boat can also vary considerably, according to the pricing structure of the travel agent or tour organization. It depends on the profit the tour company wishes to make from their enterprise.

The price that you would pay for the Islands segment of your trip ranges from about $100 U.S. per day to as high as $250. But the majority of the boats that offer good service will be at the middle of this scale, averaging about $150.00.

Your travel agent or tour organizer should be able to show you recent pictures of the available boats, including information on navigational equipment, expected itinerary (which cannot be absolutely fixed), average speed, drawings of the complete internal layout, notation on number of bunks per room, number of toilets, etc. This information is essential for your decision-making. If your agent or tour company can't provide this kind of material, *go to a different one.* Shop around for what travel agents can offer and compare with organized tours, which often have their own special emphasis. Tours may have their own tour group leaders who may be birding or natural history experts. Of course, the boat will have its own local naturalist-guide or auxiliary guide, as they all do.

The names and carrying capacities of some of the smaller boats, which are considered to be very dependable in terms of value for money, are listed below. This is about half of the number of smaller boats available. Remember, though, that boats are frequently being renovated, and personnel may change, so these names won't represent the full range of possibilities for you. It will still be a matter of checking your information, going by word of mouth, and then seeing what happens. (The * indicates a motor/sailer.)

6-passenger	*Pirata**
8-passenger	*Marigold*
	Pata Feo
	Acuario
10-passenger	*Encantada**
	*Sulidae**
	Beagle II
12-passenger	*Tip Top, Amigo, San Antonio, El Dorado*
	*Andando**

With all this discussion of prices and cabins and planning, it may sound like the whole adventure can be predicted, or that if you figure out some exact calculation of cost and space you'll know exactly what will happen. However, the Galapagos must be one of the few travel destinations where the actual *quality* of the experience is *not* largely predicated on cost. This is because the Galapagos visit is not and cannot be a totally "determined" experience. There are humans, animals, machines, weather, seasons and just plain luck all working together to shape your trip. Each boat has its captain, crew, cook and trained naturalist-guide or auxiliary guide. (The naturalist-guides have undergone a longer training period than the auxiliary guides, and usually are tri-lingual.) A good cook or a good guide—no matter which level of training—can make a trip a totally rewarding experience. The opposite is also true. But the size or cost of the boat *does not* determine the quality of the cooking or guiding or the overall experience. ❦

Physical and Mental Requirements

4

G iven the distance and potential expense of a trip like this, it is important to have a good "match" between the person and the destination. The best approximation of the overall rigors of the trip would be a two-week backpacking trip, only someone else carries your load and cooks the food. Not terribly rough, in other words, but still demanding a degree of patience and energy. The element that must be added to this is that it is *ocean* camping. That 15- to 25-meter boat is your home. Those people are your companions. That ocean is not going to go away. In terms of mental outlook, people who can roll with the punches (and the ocean swells), who like to be with people but still can find amusement in quiet reading or journal-writing in the evenings, and who love the outdoors in all its endless variety, will be very glad they went.

In physical terms, the person who is basically healthy, who can scamper up and down a ladder on the side of a heaving boat, walk a couple of hours now and then in blazing sun, withstand a chilly breeze and the slap of a wave across the face — that person will be very happy on the trip.

I would suggest that you be able to swim and generally be comfortable around water. At the very least, don't be shy about wearing a life jacket on the short trips in the little panga that ferries you between the shore and your boat.

A Word About Children

C hildren certainly do make the trip to the Galapagos. Only travel-hardened children under 10 years or so should be taken, however. Older children are more likely to enjoy themselves and not be a trial to others.

First, I would strongly suggest that children be good swimmers. They are not more likely to fall overboard than an adult, but they will probably be much more interested in swimming. It can be very restful for them to look forward to swimming in the slow times, assuming the water is warm enough. Also, it is the adult who will be responsible for them, and worrying about them, so parents should do themselves a favor and make sure the child swims well.

If the children have a highly developed sense of curiosity, are fairly patient with long boat rides where there may be "nothing to do" except sit or read or draw, and can put up with sunburn or seasickness and unfamiliar food, then bring them along. For any child under 14 or so, a week-long trip would be about their limit of physical and psychological tolerance. 🐦

What to Bring 5

The following are the basic essentials that every Galapagos visitor should bring. It is based on a two-week trip. It does not include what you might want to bring for any time you spend in mainland Ecuador or what you should bring if you are doing the hike or overnight trip up Volcan Alcedo. The overnight to Alcedo is done only by pre-arrangement and is possible only on 14-night trips. If you want to do this, you must be absolutely certain before you leave that this has been scheduled as part of your trip. Of course, once you are there, it is possible that weather conditions or other unforeseen circumstances could force you to make on-the-spot changes in your itinerary.

Clothing

2 pairs long pants, lightweight
2-3 pairs sturdy, lightweight
   shorts
1 bathing suit
1 week supply underwear
2-3 "tank tops"
2-3 short-sleeve shirts
2 long-sleeve, long-body
   lightweight shirts

1 hooded sweatshirt
1 rain jacket
1 pair slip-on plastic or cloth shoes
   for wet landings
2 pairs sturdy running shoes
2-3 pairs regular-length socks
5 pairs ankle-length socks

Toiletries, medicine

1 large towel, 1 small towel, 1 face cloth

toiletries (tooth paste, brush, tampons, facial tissues, skin conditioner cream, etc.)

sun block (as strong as possible), sunglasses

shampoo — (Used for clothes washing as well as hair. Salt water soap not necessary.)

12 large safety pins (Diaper pins ideal)

small first aid kit (band-aids, antibiotic ointment, aspirins, sunburn/abrasion cream, etc.)

medications you require (Take two sets of each if possible. Keep one set with you in your hand luggage on the plane. Pack the other. On the boat, keep the two sets in different places, and avoid carrying the whole supply with you at any one time.)

eye glasses (Take two pairs and observe the same precautions as for medications.)
anti-nausea pills

Regarding the last item: consult your physician before using scopalamine, the "stick on" medication. There have been reports of uncomfortable side effects, frequently including vision disturbances, nausea upon cessation of its use, and urinary retention in older men. Just get Dramamine-type pills and take them several hours before you sail; for the next two or three days take them every 4 hours during the day. Then test yourself without them on a short voyage. If you build it up in your system early on you should be able to avoid discomfort. Most people find they don't need any help after the first 3 or 4 days.

Equipment

W hat equipment you bring will, of course, reflect your own interests. In general, I'd suggest binoculars and camera, a small day pack for carrying film, towel, etc., when you're ashore, and an unbreakable water flask. Mask, snorkel and fins are very useful, too. Some people bring tape recorders and video equipment. Just remember that you will be getting on and off boats several times a day, so insure everything before you go and don't take anything you're not prepared to watch sink to the bottom of the ocean.

Scuba diving is a growing activity in the Islands, but it can only be done with a tour that is entirely devoted to this. The Park requires that the boat have a special guide who is licensed as a diver. The boat must book an itinerary that concentrates on the diving sites, which are somewhat different than the sites for dry-landers. Not all boats have the equipment for filling tanks, etc., so be sure to enquire and book ahead very early.

Passport

M ake a photocopy of your passport and your tickets before you leave home and leave it with your travel agent. If you lose these documents, it is now possible to have copies faxed to you, with an excellent chance that they will be treated as valid.

Money

Y ou will want $2–3 U.S. per day to pay for cold drinks and beer on the boat. And I would suggest a calculation of about 8 percent of the cost of your boat time for tips for the crew at the end of the trip. It's usually put into a kitty and given to the captain to distribute. You don't have to do it, but you probably will want to thank them in this way. The chances are you will be extremely impressed and even touched by the expert and solicitous care you receive from the captain and crew. 🍎

Notes on Photography

6

First, bring a camera and make absolutely sure you know how to use it. If you are not deeply involved with photography, one of the small, completely automatic cameras are excellent for taking scenery shots. You may not be able to do a close-up of a dozing iguana, but if there is a rock face littered with them, you can get a good picture. It will be a good camera for on-boat pictures of the group, also.

If you are an experienced photographer, then you are in for one of the most exciting photographic adventures of your life. A 35-millimeter single lens reflex camera will be your likely choice. For lenses, the essentials are a wide angle, a standard, and a moderate telephoto. If you like macro photography of plants, etc., then bring your favorite lens for that. The animal and bird life is so close that a powerful telephoto lens is quite unnecessary and just means more weight (unless you use a "mirror" lens, which is an excellent choice, given its ability to focus on objects only a meter or so away).

Above all, **bring polarizing filters for every lens**. You will be taking pictures in highly reflective conditions and on and into water most of the time. You are seriously reducing your chances of good pictures by not having these filters.

As for film, even though you are at the Equator, the Galapagos are very often under high cloud, and though you can get a great sunburn, the available light for photography is often less than you would expect. So I would suggest that you bring a wide range of film speeds.

As for the amount of film you will need, I take at least enough for two 36-exposure rolls per day. Just remember that you will be visiting two or more sites a day, you may want to take on-board shots at any time, and will need additional film if you travel on the mainland. So try to plan accordingly. Don't expect to buy film in Ecuador. It can be done, but you have no way of knowing how long it has been stored or under what conditions. So don't skimp — the Galapagos deserve your best.

Before you go, take all your film out of its boxes and mark the cartridge lids with an indelible ink, noting the film speed and number of exposures per cartridge. Then put it in a strong clear plastic bag for taking it through airport inspections. Have the bag immediately accessible so you can easily hand it over to the attendant as you approach the x-ray machines. Sometimes you find attendants who don't want to cooperate, but be ready with the bag, smile and stand firm.

◀ Close-up of red-footed booby

Male vermilion flycatcher

Be sure to bring several of these sturdy plastic bags that you can close tightly. They are good for protecting your camera during sudden rains, or for the trip between your boat and land. Once on your boat (or in the rain forest on the mainland), try to keep your film cool. On your land treks, take only the few rolls of film that you think you will use. Leave the rest in as low a location as possible in your cabin and wrap it in your clothes, dry towel, etc., to provide some insulation against the heat. Check it periodically to see that it's not heating up.

If you are able to do little repairs on your camera, then do bring the appropriate tools, especially a screwdriver that will allow general tightening of the equipment.

Be sure to start with new batteries for everything, and bring a replacement set. Also, cleaning equipment is essential. 🐦

Hood mockingbird *(Nesomimus macdonaldi)* and friend ▶

APPENDICES

A. Quito and Mainland Ecuador

I f you're planning to go as far as the Galapagos, do take the time to visit some of mainland Ecuador. Ecuador is a magnificent country, extraordinarily varied in its geography, its peoples, its natural and human history. It is beyond the scope of this book to give you detailed advice on mainland visiting, but there are books on travel in Ecuador that will be helpful. The ones aimed at backpackers often have the best information.

You will be arriving at and leaving from Quito, so at the very least spend time there. You should stay in one of the better hotels used by local people. They are often family operations, and are completely comfortable and well-served. Unless you are ready to spend the same kind of money you spend in a downtown hotel in the U.S. or Europe, for no better service, stay away from "international" hotels. They are good to visit to exchange your money or to book a car and driver for short trips, but otherwise a more modest approach to accommodation is best. Your travel agent should be able to help you here. The price range will be a good guide. (Aim for the middle.)

Also, if you book through a company that offers the boat tours, they will often be booking you into hotels in Quito. The price should be broken down at your agent's, so you can see what you are paying for and can make comparisons.

Quito is a city built during Spanish colonial times. Its Old Quarter has been designated as a World Heritage Site by UNESCO. The Old Quarter is crowded and fascinating. There are regular tours you can take there, and it is an easy walk on your own once you take a taxi from the newer section of the city, where you will likely be staying.

You will feel quite safe in terms of the courteous treatment from people, but picking pockets, or snatching cameras or purses, is becoming increasingly common in the old colonial part of the city; it's crowded there, with lots of people milling around on church steps in narrow streets. (The market towns of Otavalo and Latacunga are beginning to acquire this reputation as well, unfortunately.) So take reasonable precautions, such as carrying most of your money in a sack around your neck under your shirt, or in an extra pocket inside slacks. Don't carry free-hanging purses, or cameras attached only by a little cord to your wrist. The newer sections of town seem to have few problems of this sort.

When you are in Quito, you are very likely to suffer a bit from the effects of suddenly arriving at high altitudes: headaches, tiring from the briefest of quick walks, nausea and difficulty in sleeping. These symptoms will go away as soon as the traveler gets to sea level; acclimatization to Quito itself will occur within two or three days for most people. By walking slowly, eating moderately and resting often, you should have little difficulty. The one other thing you might want to consider is taking a few sleeping pills for your Quito stay. Altitude sometimes makes people very restive, and the city is quite noisy at night, particularly if you are in one of the small hotels or pensions in semi-residential areas. (I think every house has a barking German shepherd on guard.)

An absolute must for a two- or three-day trip out of Quito is an excursion to one of the beautiful historic haciendas in the area; some are only a two-hour drive from the capital. They are in the Highlands and give a dazzling experience of the Andes. I stayed at two different haciendas not far from Quito.

In both cases the haciendas were beautifully renovated, completely comfortable inns. All meals were included. There were plenty of places to walk in the countryside, horseback riding was available, the hosts were very helpful. The cost is about $50 U.S. per night per person, all included. (This is the maximum you should have to pay for any hotel in Ecuador.) Ask your travel agent, or one in Quito, about booking a stay in one of these beautiful places.

The cloud forest on the western slope of the Andes, only a few hours' drive from Quito or Guayaquil, is a paradise for bird-watchers. There are several hotels and lodges there that cater to their needs. "Tinalandia," near Santo Domingo de los Colorados, is a one-of-a-kind institution, world-famed among birders.

It is possible to take trips into the Amazonas area, a rich sweep of rain forest that clothes the eastern side of the Ecuadorean Andes. Your travel agent may be able to help you make arrangements, or a nature club or nature tour organization may run tours from your home city. I would suggest pre-booking if possible, but you can book a trip on one of the "flotels" (floating hotels) on the Rio Napo, or similar trips, once you are in Quito. Ask at your hotel how to contact the agent. If you leave yourself several days in Quito before your departure for the Galapagos, you should be able to reserve a trip for when you return. The usual duration of one of these trips is four or five days.

SOME SUMMARY COMMENTS ON TRAVEL IN ECUADOR

If overall impressions can be depended upon, I can unequivocally state that in my three visits and six weeks in the Ecuadorean mainland, there was only one time when I was not made to feel completely welcome, safe, comfortable, and fairly and openly treated in all financial exchanges.

I traveled on a modest scale, using good, locally patronized hotels and pensions. They may have been fairly expensive by local standards, but were quite reasonable for a North American. I was with a large group on one trip, though we often went off on our own in groups of two or three. I took taxis and walked around Quito, and took buses to Tinalandia and back, with a woman friend. I also booked a car and driver for three days on one of my stays in a hacienda (which cost $80 U.S. a day), to save time and to have a bilingual guide available at all times for side trips for birding or climbing.

The one exception to easy travel was when a very young and officious local "immigration officer" came up to our group in a village square and asked for our identification. Our guide came up quickly and put a stop to the questions with a burst of outraged Spanish.

And speaking of Spanish: if you know how to count to 10 and then by hundreds, can use standard pleasantries for time of day, for the bill ("la cuenta, por favor"), and "thank you" and "please," and you are prepared to smile on any and every occasion when things go a little more slowly than you expect, you will be fine. The firm, almost authoritarian approach that gets things done in North America or Europe is completely ineffective in Ecuador. Smile and throw yourself on people's mercy, and their deeply ingrained politeness and kindness will have an opportunity to express itself fully.

B. Suggested Reading

Note: at one of the Libri Mundi bookstores in Quito or Guayaquil you should be able to find a guidebook to the fish of the Galapagos, which Libri Mundi have published themselves. I have not seen it, but am told it is very useful for snorkelers or scuba divers.

Darwin, Charles. *The Voyage of the Beagle.* The Natural History Library, Anchor Books, Doubleday and Company, Inc., Garden City, New York, 1962.

Harris, Michael. *A Field Guide to the Birds of Galapagos,* revised edition. Collins, London, 1982.

Hickman, John. *The Enchanted Islands: The Galapagos Discovered.* Tanager Books, Dover, New Hampshire, 1985.

Jackson, Michael H. *Galapagos, A Natural History Guide.* University of Calgary Press, Calgary, Alberta, Canada, 1985.

Moore, Tui De Roy. *Galapagos: Islands Lost in Time.* The Viking Press, New York, 1980.

Nelson, Bryan. *Galapagos: Islands of Birds,* Longmans, London, 1968.

Perry, R. *Galapagos.* Pergamon Press, Oxford, 1984.

Schofield, Eileen K. *Plants of the Galapagos Islands.* Universe Books, New York, 1984.

Thornton, Ian. *Darwin's Islands: A Natural History of the Galapagos.* The Natural History Press, Garden City, New York, 1971.

C. Information for Galapagos supporters

T he Charles Darwin Foundation for the Galapagos Islands is supported by several national and international institutions but nevertheless remains largely dependent on the generosity of individual donors for the funds needed to finance its programs.

In the United States, contributions, which should be accompanied by a note indicating that they are to be used *"for conservation and science in the Galapagos Islands",* may be made out to the following organizations who support these programs:

Smithsonian Institution, c/o Secretary for the Americas (Administration), P.O. Box 37481—OBC, Washington DC 20013.

World Wildlife Fund, 1250 Twenty-fourth Street, N.W., Washington DC 20037.

U.S. citizens contributing through either of these organizations are entitled to tax reductions. No administrative fees or overheads are charged.

In Canada, you can do the same by writing to World Wildelife Fund, 60 St. Claire, #201, Toronto, Ontario M5 T 1N5. 🐦

Trip Log

	BIRDS	MAMMALS	FISH
DAY 1			
DAY 2			
DAY 3			
DAY 4			
DAY 5			
DAY 6			
DAY 7			
DAY 8			
DAY 9			
DAY 10			
DAY 11			
DAY 12			
DAY 13			
DAY 14			

PLANTS	REPTILES	OTHER NOTES, SITES VISITED, ETC.

Index

Italic = *scientific names*
Boldface = **photos**

MARYLEE STEPHENSON, a Vancouver, B.C. resident, has made numerous trips to the Galapagos and extensively interviewed both Parks Service Staff and Charles Darwin Research Station scientists to prepare this guide. Stephenson operates her own social-policy consulting firm, with special interest in environmental impact, recreation and tourism issues. She has done a number of studies for the Canadian federal agency Parks Canada; she also teaches nature photography as well as writing and lecturing in the field.

*   *   *

Other books from The Mountaineers you'll enjoy:

BICYCLING TOURING IN NEW ZEALAND, Including Both North and South Islands, by J.B. Ringer. Complete background information and detailed tours.

A GUIDE TO TREKKING IN NEPAL, 5th Edition, by Stephen Bezruchka. Information on country and culture vital for all types of travelers, plus extensively detailed route information for a wide variety of trekking routes.

PADDLING HAWAII: An Insider's Guide to Exploring the Secluded Coves, Jungle Streams & Wild Coasts of the Hawaiian Islands, by Audrey Sutherland. Full details for exploring coasts and rivers of all major islands, by kayak, canoe or inflatable.

For catalog, ordering information, write or call
The Mountaineers Books
306 Second Ave. W., Seattle, WA 98119
1-800-553-4453